The Falklands War

The Falklands War
From Defeat to Victory

A Personal Account From a Royal Marine

John Alden

Prominent Books

Editing & Layout: Writer Services, LLC (WriterServices.net)

ISBN 10: 1-942389-11-6
ISBN 13: 978-1-942389-11-8

Prominent Books and the Prominent Books logo are Trademarks of Prominent Books, LLC

Table of Contents

PART I: HUMBLE BEGINNINGS

Chapter 1
Through the Tall Grass

I remember that it was quite early. In my memory, I know that it was the morning of the second of April when the fighting first began. The year was 1982.

I was only a young lad way back then. I was still wet behind the ears. It's funny to think back on some of the things I did, especially now that I am much older.

I was just nineteen years old when I had my first taste of combat.

Looking back on those events though, and recalling how everything played out over those manic two and a half months in the Falklands, it is still hard to get my head around them. There is a framed picture on my wall, and quite a few more black and whites, and yellowed newspaper clippings, in the dusty old photo album that I have managed to hang onto through the years. Still, even when I have those images to guide me, a great deal of those details comes across as blurry. Some of the names and faces are hard to arrive at, even when I sit down quietly and grasp around in my mind for them.

Some things, however, a man simply does not forget. Perhaps it's that he cannot. Every single one of us has something, maybe even a few moments from their past, that they simply cannot bring themselves to let go of.

Growing old is partly a process of making sense of those before you go crazy. For me, a great many of those moments took place back in 1982.

I had recently enlisted in the British Marine Corps. I had already achieved a Green Beret. When you reach that level, it means you are part of something special. I was part of a small detachment of NP8901, a unit recently stationed on East Falkland. Maybe I had indeed heard of the Falkland Islands before choosing to go there, but I don't recall. Either way, they meant nothing special to me.

The other lads and I had been stationed on the islands, at our barracks, in an area called Moody Brook for only a few days. There's not a lot out there—just a main road. Directly to the east, the boggy grass gave way to a body of water. We didn't know our way around. The largest town, Stanley, we hadn't even gotten our bearings there. We had not even grown accustomed to the dubiously harsh weather conditions yet.

Our assignment was supposed to be peaceful. We were part of a simple rotation, coming in as the replacement detachment for the lads that had been stationed down there for the months before us. By late in March, though, we had all been made well aware that at least some fighting was imminent. There was tension in the air. Aggressive overtures by the Argentine army revealed that they stood on the brink of invasion, ready to take back the islands that they thought were rightfully theirs.

It was around 3 P.M. local time, on the previous day, when the other shoe finally dropped on us. It was on a Thursday, April the first when Rex Hunt, British Governor of the Falkland Islands, received an ominous telex from Military Intelligence.

We have apparently reliable evidence that an Argentine task force will gather off Cape Pembroke early tomorrow morning, 2nd April.

You will wish to make your dispositions accordingly.

I was still a fresh face beneath my proud Green Beret. I had yet to engage in any combat during my short Marine career, but I knew what the intelligence call meant. Making our dispositions was a military euphemism for "Get the boys ready to fight."

Every one of us made the same translation. This was not the first message either. Days earlier, an intercepted message to the Argentine submarine Santa Fe revealed that a few of the South American reconnaissance troops would be landing on the beach at Mullet Creek, roughly fifteen kilometers down the road from where we stood.

Later on, our detachment sorted out the news while kicking around in a local tavern near our barracks. As I remember, the boys from NP8901 were there, along with twenty Royal Navy personnel. Every one of us was rapt with attention, listening as Boss Major Mike Norman pepped us up with a forceful plan of action.

Our Major was a strident man. We had already seen that he was given to stormy fits of bluster. His words as he paced back and forth came across as urgent and forceful.

To anyone who was listening, what came next was as clear as a bell.

"Today you are going to die," he roared ominously at the sea of blank faces staring back in his direction. "So go out there and do the job you were trained to do."

My heart sank a little bit. I was not ready to die. As I glanced sideways over at the chap next to me, a medic whose face was already as pale as a ghost, I realized that he felt the same way.

I was only nineteen years old. Could this really be the end? There was nothing to be done, though, no protest. The order had been given. Now it was time to act.

A mixed mood took hold of the room. A somber air captivated some of the faces, while others were aroused, seemingly ready to relish the coming fight. As Norman finished his rallying of the boys, the meeting broke up and everyone fell in line.

I bucked up, grabbing my kit and machine gun. One of my mates, Gaz, quipped as we hurried to join our section.

"No point in getting your head down now," he said.

Gaz was right.

This is my story, but as it turns out, it is there in the history books too. I was one of those frightened lads in that dingy bar at Moody Brook barracks. We were the last and only line of defense. All that stood between the Falkland Islands, a British territory for more than a century, was in our ability to repel an uncertain army of invaders.

All of the Royal Marines abandoned the barracks at Moody Brook at roughly 0200 hours on April 2nd. Within minutes, they were empty.

Governor Hunt, a Royal Air Force flyer who fought in World War II, and led diplomatic campaigns in Malaysia, Turkey, India, and Brunei, wouldn't give up easy. He took his family, and the hand full of staff he kept, and fled Government House in the central town of Stanley to a safer location. As we moved out to our positions, the seat of British government became the temporary base of operations for defense of the islands.

Each of the six sections was designated for a specific position at a different defensive focal point on the island. Intelligence had led Major Norman to the belief that the invading Argentine army would go straight for Port Stanley, away from the city. As an attack point, the largest settlement on the island seemed a natural start, but the seat of government was also of tremendous strategic value. If Argentine forces could secure the area around the city, they would have control of the largest airstrip, and the harbor, to further secure their foothold, so our defenses were spread out accordingly.

Vehicles were ordered to park on the airstrip; they would render it all but useless for landing aircraft. A few smaller units of men were situated directly to the south; two machine gun crews set up east of Yorke point, weapons trained on the waters of the nearby bay, which seemed a likely landing place for troops and supplies. Each of the individual gun nests was equipped with a canoe and motorcycles for a quick getaway.

Section one was placed a short distance south of section five. The half dozen troops stacked up along the road leading out from the airfield toward Port Stanley, where it makes a hard, right-angled turn at what was known as Hooker's Point.

Near the old airstrip due west, section two was placed. This position was armed with a massive 84mm anti-tank weapon and 66mm anti-tank missiles. There was an old air navigation beacon nearby; section three was sent there, their orders to delay the enemy for as long as possible before eventually falling back into a secondary position.

Section four was also armed with an 84mm anti-tank gun

and they slotted in on the opposite side of Stanley Harbor, ready to take on any Argentine landing craft, or whatever ships would attempt the tight passage through the harbor's narrow entrance.

Section six, set up on Murray Heights, was ready to engage with Argentine invaders should they approach Stanley from the south. An observation point was set up on Sapper Hill. Only one Marine was sent up there to keep watch. His name, if I recall correctly, was Mike. Mike would keep an eye all around, and if he saw anything, his orders were to sound the alarm and escape on his motorcycle as quickly as possible.

When all of the British land troops were finally in place, the motor vessel Forrest was sent out onto the rough seas. Equipped with radar, it would keep watch over Port William and the dark waters to the north.

Military life ends up being a lot about waiting around. Hurry up and wait. Ninety-nine percent of a soldier's life is quite tedious, spent lingering on word. Get into position and wait. As the morning of April 2nd crept through the anxious small hours, every one of us in NP8901 did precisely that. We waited on word of our engagement with the invaders. Then, finally, that word came down.

It was 0230, only a short half-hour after we left Moody Brook, that our eyes in the sea, the MV Forrest, detected the approaching enemy; by 0330, it was obvious that a significant Argentine fleet was maneuvering off of Cape Pembrooke.

An hour later, Mike saw a few helicopters approach and land close to Mullet Creek. Word began to spread like wild fire throughout the sections. The invaders were the elite Argentine Special Forces, the troops known as Buzo Tactico, had landed on the shores southwest of Stanley, near another settlement, Port Harriet.

They rumbled in larger numbers onto land, past Walebone Cove in a line of LVTP-7's, Amtrak personnel carriers. There were eighteen of the impressive American-made vehicles, each loaded with troops and equipped with .30 caliber machine guns.

The one hundred and twenty man invading force moved slowly up toward Sapper Hill before breaking off into two separate parties: the first moved into the hills, rounding back behind Government House, while the other headed directly toward the Marine barracks at Moody Brook, where they made their first, vicious attack.

By a little after six in the morning, those barracks where we had been given our orders were ablaze. The Buzo Tactico had been hopeful of catching us sleeping. They saturated the structure with heavy machine gun fire and phosphorous grenades. The attack was successful in destroying the structure, but they had arrived too late.

If the attack had come any earlier, the result would have been devastating.

As the Moody Brook barracks burned to the ground a few kilometers northwest of Stanley, the attacking Argentine troops turned and began a trek toward the city. The unit that had first split into two halves would converse back together as one, clamping down like a vice around Government House.

The Marines had been successful in avoiding devastation at Moody Brook, but by now, Major Norman had to recognize what was going on. The Marine forces were outnumbered and badly outgunned. The guys in section two managed to pick off one of the Argentine LVTP-7's. A sharp-eyed marine managed to get off a shot from an anti-armor weapon, striking the passenger compartment. Others opened fire on the Amtrak, stopping it in its tracks. Section two may have slowed down the advancing vehicle, but this only served to make things worse. A fleet of Argentine vehicles emptied their troops, giving them cover as they moved forward, machine guns blasting.

As dawn crept closer, skirmishes like these broke out all over the island. The Marines fiercely engaged the invaders. The determined soldiers fought as long and as valiantly as they could. Backs against the walls though, each movement seemed to send them scrambling for a new position while the Argentine invaders dug in and fortified.

Scattered gunfire was exchanged between riflemen. Here and there, a lucky sniper caught a foot soldier, racing through the morning. British forces were able to fight in brief, intense periods, but they only managed to delay the advance before falling back. Our purpose was to defend the islands for as long as possible, either to repel them or scatter them far enough to regroup; we were largely unsuccessful on both fronts.

Major Norman had been caught with his pants down. All of the British troop positions were defending against an attack from the northeast; the Argentines had invaded the island from the opposite direction. Quickly, Norman called sections one and five back into Stanley and ordered them to retreat all the way back to Government House, where he too would hole up and prepare for his next move.

At 0615, the second branch of the Buzo Tactico party began

their attack on the Government House complex. Argentine soldiers came down from the hills, approaching through a field at the rear of the complex. Six actually made it that far and made a bold attempt to enter the rear of Government House. Three were shot dead by defending Marines; the other three hid out in the Maid's Quarters in an outbuilding behind the main house. The hand full of Marines in the building managed to repel the rest of the Buzo Tactico, holding them off with rifle and machine gun fire.

Norman had made a request for support, but only roughly five minutes had passed since his call; not nearly enough time for sections one and five to help secure headquarters. Another wave of Argentine attackers, and the building could fall.

Gunfire volleyed all around the old building. As Norman scrambled back into the building, he found he was cut off. There were only thirty-one Royal Marines, eleven sailors from the HMS Endurance, and an ex-Marine named Jim Fairfield left to defend the entire seat of government on the Falkland Islands. Between gunfire bursts, they could hear shouts in the trees. The next wave of Argentine forces drew nearer.

As the sun rose, the British position could be delicately described as precarious.

I was one of the gunners in the group designated as section one. I took a spot on the side of the road near Gaz, the second on my gun. We lay, elbows down in the cold, rough gravel and began scanning the area for Argentine troops. As far as we knew, our attackers could come from any direction.

We had spent those hours in the dark, watching for troop

movement. It wasn't long before I was utterly exhausted. I heard Spanish voices throughout the night, men traipsing through the tussock grass and boggy water.

Once those few scattered voices broke off, there was silence; again, our orders were to wait, with our guns trained and senses alert.

After what seemed an eternity waiting, I nodded off. Finally, our radio, which was supposed to remain silent, burst to life. Orders for our movement were delivered.

Gaz whispered to me, "Radio message from Fleetwood intelligence, good luck."

Good fucking luck, I thought.

With the other six members of section one, I climbed into the back of a waiting Land Rover. When everyone was finally settled, we were ready to move. We would be heading down the road, back toward Stanley. We were quiet; there was an eerie feeling in the air, even amongst the old sweats in the section that had seen a few fire fights before and survived to tell about it.

I felt a stream of adrenaline begin to course through my blood; I felt my senses heightening, becoming sharper, honing in with each passing second. The Land Rover's headlights were turned off as we moved. All we could see up ahead was tracer ammunition racing across the sky. We were headed into the very teeth of the conflict.

The sun was nowhere near cracking the eastern horizon as section one arrived at our tactical position. We were only a short distance south from where command had placed the fifth section; we could almost shout to one another we were so close together. Our position was approaching the port, a place that I had still yet to visit in the course of my short deployment. As my fellow Marines and I got out of the Land Rover and it backed away up the road, a disoriented feeling overwhelmed me.

As we got ourselves situated, we received word from command back at Sink Fleet in England. Good luck, they said.

Translation, you're on your own.

Then radio silence. Everything seemed to pass before my eyes in a blur. I saw figures pass my line of sight. They were hallucinations—I knew this because although I saw something move, I couldn't hear anything above the howling gusts of autumn wind.

From every direction around Gaz and I, we heard sporadic exchanges of machine gun fire. There were a few shell bursts too, but whose ordinance was exploding, and precisely where it landed, we could not tell.

Our section commander, Lou, took his position close to us as the Land Rover vanished into the morning. As far as I could tell, somewhere during what amounted to a short span of time, the corporal had been in contact with command.

Finally, radio silence broke and Lou lurched forward. "We're going back to Stanley," he shouted at the top of his lungs, struggling to cut his words in over the constant howl. "Come on, those bastards may already be there by now."

We didn't know it at the time, but our order was the call for troop support from Major Mike Norman. The Argentines were closing in on them at Government House.

Silence lingered. Everything but the wind seemed unnaturally still. Then I saw Gaz scramble forward, running down the road.

Then in a split second, I was up and close on his heels. Major Norman's words hung heavy over me as I disappeared down that road toward the waiting Land Rover.

"Today you are going to die," he had said. "So go out there and do the job you're trained to do."

On my back, I carried a general-purpose machine gun. It was a beastly weapon, what the Marines casually referred to as the GPMG. In addition to the usual combat kit, my pack was loaded up with over two thousand rounds of 7.62 ammunition; it was an oppressively heavy load, even for a battle trained Marine in the best shape, who had run thousands of kilometers in training. Even aided by the adrenaline of an oncoming firefight coursing through my blood, it was a bloody awkward weapon to carry around.

As the Land Rover slowed to a stop at the edge of town, the scene was quite impressive, like something out of Apocalypse Now. The whole sky was lit up with tracers and explosions. The sight was enough to take your breath away, even from an old sweat.

All throughout that short drive from our first position, I remember wondering what I would do when I came under enemy fire. Would I freeze up?

Would I shit myself out of fear?

Everyone in my section stepped outside. With our backs to the vehicle, we walked a circle around to be sure we were in a safe position.

Then Lou staggered out onto the road. It was time to get a move on.

We knew where we were supposed to end up, but we had no idea how to get around Stanley. We didn't have any maps. It was still dark outside. We were guided by feel, trusting our instinct, our ears directing us toward the sounds of combat. All we had was a vague compass bearing that would supposedly lead to Government House.

The side streets and alleys in Stanley were barely lit. There were no lights on in the houses, no streetlights filling in the sidewalk shadows. The periodic explosions overhead and tracer fire were hardly enough to see what was going on. There were a few parked cars and some shop signs. There were a few signs of life, as it had been on the day before the invasion. When I think back on those streets though, I don't recall seeing any citizens out or in hiding.

There may have been though, I don't know. Adrenaline had taken over. My focus had become precariously narrow.

Section one moved together though, in tactical sync, through the streets. I would race forward across an open street or down a block and open fire. I would fill the darkness with bursts of gunfire, lighting up anywhere an enemy soldier might be hiding. I would cover long enough for the rest of the section to move forward. When they were in position, I would get the signal, and then I would follow and catch up.

We moved rather slowly, but the strategy got us safely through the streets. Still, after some time racing through the chaotic scene in Stanley, we had no idea where Government House was, and it wasn't until we ran into someone from section two that we found someone who did.

We were turned around. He pointed us in the right direction.

My machine gun was bloody heavy, but each round that I fired made it feel slightly lighter and easier to manage. Maybe I was kidding myself, but after lighting up a street corner with a loud burst of fire from that barrel, its weight became easier to manage. A gun like that one gives power to the shooter—every Marine wants to hold it, claim its glory. I fed off of the GPMG.

After some time, Government House came into sight. We were only a short distance away. After a few blocks, we had reached the gardens of a nearby house, surrounded by a wooden fence.

We crouched down as low as we could. With our backs to the fence, for the first time in a while, everything was in front of us. This seemed like the perfect place to gather our wits. We each drew a breath and got our bearings. We could see that the quickest route up to Government House was down a vanishing path directly over the fence that was at least shoulder height.

Suddenly, in ebb of adrenaline, the weight of the gun and ammo took a heavy toll on me. "I'm fucked," I said, gasping for breath.

Gaz looked around and quickly came up with a plan.

"You give me the gun," he said.

Immediately, I recoiled. That was my weapon, giving it up was a foolish idea.

"No, listen to me, John," he said. "I'll take it so that way, you can jump over the fence and I'll hand it to you."

I nodded. With cat like agility, I leaped over the fence and a spray of gunfire appeared, blowing holes in the wood where, only seconds ago, my legs had been.

"Alright," Gaz said, reaching down for the gun.

His hand wrapped around the metal as he picked it up. He then screamed out in terrible pain as he tossed it over to me.

Gaz's pained howls were awful. My first thought was that the same Argentine gunman that had narrowly missed taking off my legs had shot him. When I glanced down to assess the damage though, I could see why he screamed. The barrel of the gun he had just tossed over the fence, and had fired off more than a thousand rounds of ammunition out of, was sizzling hot, enough to have burned most of the skin off of his hand on contact. I had not had enough wherewithal to caution Gaz that he should pick the gun up properly, by its tripod.

I helped Gaz over the fence. There was no time for licking wounds though. A spray of bullets in the gut would be far worse than a flesh wound.

I remember that beyond the fence, we raced through a garden. In that strangely tranquil place, we met up with the rest of the lads from section two. They were responding to the same order of retreat to Government House that we were.

Through the garden, we arrived at a football pitch. The manicured field of lush green grass seemed strange, spread wide out in front of us. Across that open space appeared to be the quickest path into Government House. The rest of section one was right on our heels. Orders came up from Lou, who had fallen in behind the section. Two at a time, he said. Pepper pot your way across to evade enemy fire.

I was aghast at Lou's command. Gaz, whose shredded hand was dripping blood, could not believe his ears. The order to cross felt like a blind suicide run. There were hundreds of uncovered meters between where we were and the next hiding place.

Orders were orders, though. However absurd or suicidal they may seem, the Green Beret meant it was your sworn duty to do what you're told.

With my weapon in hand, I ran forward. Every moment crossing that pitch felt like it took place in a surreal, dream like state. Gaz was beside me. Gunfire rained down all around us. I could see a hedgerow rise before me, a place the section could slot in. That's where I would run to, the hedgerow on a track that led around into the building.

Then I slammed into the bush. Sweat poured into my eyes and down my face as I drew a few quick breaths. Within seconds, all twelve soldiers had fallen in behind me.

Gaz shot me a grin. Then he winced and shook his head gratefully. Everyone in section one and two had survived and I was, for a moment, in the lead position.

Standing in the distant rear of our formation, Lou leaned out and hastily signaled for me to move forward. "Go," he shouted. "And John, fire if anyone fires at you."

Fear coursed through my body as I crept forward for the corner of the hedgerow. None of us knew what was around the corner.

In the heat of a firefight, two factors must take hold in order for a soldier to survive the ordeal. The first is an ability to push through exhaustion and pain, or a shot of adrenaline; the second is the ability to seamlessly access their training.

Doing both in tandem is a matter of survival. Every one of the Marines lined up along that hedgerow was utterly exhausted. No one had really slept. Gaz's flesh was still cooking on my hot gun barrel; his red and bleeding hand was obviously in intense pain.

Neither of those factors could affect our plunge forward

though. Bloody hand or not, neither Gaz nor anyone else could tap out now.

A soldier's body and mind cannot stand as separate entities; they must unite into a sharp focus. Their concert stands as their best chance to live and tell the combat story tomorrow. All of the younger guys in our section had heard the stories from a few of the older Marines. They'd fought in Ireland, Asia, and Africa. Staying calm and focused would be our way to tell the story of the battle for the Falkland Islands one day.

As I have said, I was green. I was only a few hours into my first firefight. Still, everything I had done in the military had led up to the point where Lou told me that I was leading section one's charge into Government House. This was what I trained for.

Everything I had done was part of the long process of proving to myself, and my mates, that I was capable of enduring and thriving in this moment.

Government House is a mass of cold, gray stone. By European standards, the surrounding grounds are modest; however, the structure stands as one of the largest in the entire South Atlantic. From a distance, Government House resembles something like an old English country mansion, with gardens and a slated green roof, the north pitch of which faces the icy cold waters of Blanco Bay, which lies only a few hundred yards away. Off the northeast corner of the property is the peninsula where the Stanley airport was situated. Someone sitting in the front row of windows could see all the ships and planes coming into Stanley.

Government House had been the seat of governors ruling the Falkland Islands since it was first constructed back in 1845. In the hundred and thirty-seven years since, it had been host to any traveling English dignitary passing through on business.

Some would say that was anyone unfortunate enough to land on the islands. Sir Ernest Shackleton, who had been a pioneer in Arctic exploration, described his time there as being "colder than any time on the ice."

There was no one else around. It felt as though we had been separated from the other sections. We could also see that we were badly outnumbered. The noose that had been tossed around our heads by the Buzo Tactico was rapidly tightening. Our hope was to find Major Norman still alive in Government House. Shelter there would be our last chance at survival. There was nowhere else for section one to turn to.

Moving first off the hedgerow, I encountered a cold silence in the immediate vicinity. I could see that the curtains in the windows closest to me were open, but inside was dark. Everything felt rather dour in the morning light.

Government House was either already abandoned, or a trap.

We moved our way around the corner and up the path. Again, nothing moved. The idea of daylight was almost meaningless in a place so dim, so cold. Still, I could see nothing that informed me to duck, move forward, or fire my machine gun.

So, I put one foot in front of another and continued creeping forward. I don't know whether I was holding my breath or not, but I remember everything felt suspended, out of time; I was waiting for the thump of a round hitting my body.

Once sections one and two were all the way inside of the complex, we faced a low brick wall, beyond which was a courtyard. There, we were confronted by three dead bodies strewn about. They were shot up, faces down, the first dead bodies I had seen. I held my breath; at first glance, I couldn't tell whose they were, theirs or ours.

We got closer. I was relieved that they were Argentine soldiers. But at the time, we did not know how they had gotten there. Had those three soldiers died as the Buzo Tactico took Government House? Or were they part of a unit that had been repulsed.

A strange twinge of confidence made its way through me. Something told me that we had fought them off.

We drew closer to what appeared to be a kitchen. The windows were dark. The door, still intact, was closed tight. Still not certain whether or not the building was in enemy or friendly hands, everyone drew in another step closer behind me and tensed.

I fixed my grip firmly on the weapon. My finger flexed before finding the trigger again, making sure I was ready, should my reflex tell me to fire.

Under the awning, I could see my reflection coming up into the window. A voice shouted out, "Royal marines."

I startled but managed to keep my gun barrel held eerily still. Now full, my reflection stared back at me in the darkened window.

Then there was movement inside; although slight, everyone tensed.

My finger pressed. Every bit of me prepared to open fire. All that came next was an awful blur as the guys in section one blew past me through the kitchen door, where the frightened face of a fellow Royal Marine looked back.

"Come on," he shouted at us, and motioned all of us into safety.

Gun lowered, I ran in, grateful to finally see another friendly face.

Chapter 2
Operation Corporate

I remember when I knew I would enlist in the military. The young man that walked through those doors was so immature, a baby practically, at least compared to the lad that stormed through that back door of Government House.

I remember that I paraded straight into the recruitment office in my city. In the lobby, I saw a picture on the wall. I thought to myself, I want to do that right there, not really being certain what that fully meant at the time.

When the time finally arrived and I was of age, that is precisely what I did. Home was a broken place, providing no refuge for self-exploration. Mom had moved out, desperate to get away from Dad; I had not seen my sister in an age. I was without an anchor, so I made one for myself. I signed myself over to the Royal British Marines. I received my instructions to be at Lympstone Commando training center, 23rd July 1979, giving me a couple of weeks to blow off steam and wreak havoc in the local villages. Two weeks felt like forever.

Looking back, it is strange to think of how simple even the most fundamental decisions in our lives turn out to be. I saw a bloody picture. I recall how its heroic image struck me. That's all it took; I was sold.

However sudden it may have seemed, the decision made a

great deal of sense. Given the choice of a hard life scrapping or fighting, or fighting for some purpose, I made the choice to go out and fight for my country.

Growing up in the village, I was the son of a working class man. We were from the countryside. For generations, my whole family had to work their fingers to the bone in order to even scratch out a living. I was a good-looking guy, or at least I thought that I was. I never had much trouble with the young ladies.

My father worked as a miner for most of his life. He was a rough sort of guy, the kind of man who went deep into the earth to feed his family, and when he got back home at the end of the day, he often didn't come back out.

I was an ornery kid, stubborn, bull headed. Dad gave me more than my share of whippings. He talked to me in hard, unforgiving tones.

I don't know what Dad was so angry about. Maybe there was something, and just as likely, maybe there was nothing at all. Maybe he was just a mean sort.

Either way, I knew that working six days a week, going down and coming out of that mine, wasn't the life for me. I would do something different.

England was a different country back then, in the 1970's. The whole world seemed much different as well. The Iron Lady, Margaret Thatcher, had been in office for a few years, and the country was mired in the midst of a difficult recession.

I was a teenager during the Winter of Discontent, the cold, conflict filled months bridging 1978 and 1979. There were riots and strikes. Trade unions demanded pay raises in the face of wage caps. The Labor Party pushed back, breaking their contracts as a way of controlling inflation, which was on the brink of spiraling out of control. They came down hard on public employees and openly urged private employers to follow.

Refuse collectors went on strike. Liverpool gravediggers wouldn't work. Emergency medical workers lined up outside of hospitals, barricading entrances.

What made things even worse was that those few months were the coldest in more than fifteen years. There were record-breaking snows in every part of the country. The streets were choked off with ice. As a result of fear and government paralysis, retail spending plummeted around Christmas. Shops closed. Things appeared terribly bleak.

I remember that there was a lot of "us and them" talk going around in England when I was a teenager. Even after the thaw, jobs remained scarce. Everyone stayed on edge. Punk rock exploded on the scene. There was a constant scent of fury in the air.

Even in the backwater villages around Nottinghamshire, punk's frantic wail could be heard from the run down clubs and dingy concert halls. We had a place back home where bands played frequently, Grey Topper. The reeking old converted cinema, with its carpet and nicotine stained ceiling, was the center of my life in those days leading up to departure. The space was cramped, and in the warmer months, it got quite humid; during a show, the air was alive with volatile energy. Front and center on stage were the queer, abrasive, punk rock Gods, guitars blaring, screaming at the top of their lungs.

It was a brutal sort of heaven for a lad like me.

I remember the U.K. Subs played a few shows in the summer

of 1979. One of those was at the Grey Topper, scheduled the night before I left for my journey.

That night, the scene was typical. There was a lot of spitting at the band. Fist-fights broke out everywhere, even between sets. I strutted through the mosh pit, weaving in and out of the pogo dancers as Chris Harper belted out his vocals. He was pissed. I could feel it. I was pissed off too. I was ready to leave this shit hole town forever.

In the midst of the U.K. Subs set, my head near the stack of speakers, I got a friendly tap on the shoulder. I turned around to find it was a girl from school, Paula. She was a year younger but luscious. I can still see her now, all these years later.

Paula knew I was leaving town, and in that ear splitting moment, decided to give me a gift to show me how much she would miss seeing me. Paula dropped to her knees, eyes lowering as she unzipped my pants, and went to town.

What was I supposed to do? Right there, in front of the band and the sea of pogo punks, I closed my eyes and let her go. It was the best blowjob I'd had, or would ever.

The ringing in my ears continued as I woke up and it lasted well into my journey down to Exmouth the next day. It was my first day of training.

There wasn't a lot in the way of upward mobility for average guys like my Dad. Seemed like he would always struggle to carve out a living, however hard he worked.

The way I saw it, the process of figuring out who the "haves" and "have-nots" were in society seemed altogether rigged.

There is a natural sorting out that takes place in the military. It's not a very subtle process, but the pecking order must be established.

As a soldier, if you made it through basic training, odds are, you were the toughest guy from your school or town. The lad next to you was the toughest guy in his school too, and so was the guy next to him, and so on and so on. In a unit full of tough necks, where everyone was a brash alpha male, the process of sorting out often lacks all the elements of nuance.

Everyone strutted around the barracks, or while out on leave, with a whole hell of a lot to prove. Who they had to prove themselves to was entirely up to them. There was not a single Royal Marine among us who was accustomed to taking a step down, so whenever provoked or otherwise tested, you had no choice but to prove to the guy whose fists were raised and lips curled hatefully that you belonged in the ring with him.

Proving yourself came down in one of two ways, fighting being first. The other way was drinking. A Marine had to be proficient in either one.

Odds were, however, that the two ways went hand in hand. I spent a countless lot of those early days in uniform, fighting and drinking my way through life.

When the dust settled, we Marines had to prove ourselves worthy in another pursuit, which we called "trapping." We were relentless in trying to score with the ladies. Everywhere we went was a process of talking tough, drinking a lot of whatever we could get our hands on, and then finding someone to trap.

My appetite for women was voracious. I chased them like medals. I was relentless from the moment I was enlisted in the Commandos.

In a lot of ways, looking back on those rough, early days,

I can see now that every one of us went through life with blinders on.

Maybe I knew this much going in, and maybe I did not.

Either way, the path to surviving my time in the Marines was clear. I would have to fight my way through. I had taken beatings, more than my share. More often than not, though, I doled out a good whipping too.

I wasn't afraid of what proving myself boiled down to.

I wasn't an ambitious type of recruit. As I came into my own as a soldier and a man, I didn't have my sights set on moving up. Unlike some of the others, I wasn't bent on becoming a general, or a major, or even a corporal. I wanted to survive.

For guys like me, being in the military stood for something. I wasn't going to school. There wasn't a career in business or medicine for me. Maybe I would score with the ladies using my charm, but I found out fast that a uniform goes further.

I wanted to belong to a cause bigger than myself. The Marines gave that to me.

More than anything else, on a much deeper and far more personal level, I did not want to go down into the mine like Dad did. I was not going to live my life underground. I wanted to see the world. I would defend England.

Life in the late 1970s was pretty cut and dried, especially for guys like me. Enlist in the military, or else find your own hard scrabbled way, all alone.

Half way across the world, in Argentina, life for its citizens was much the same. They were living restless, stagnant lives, bereft of opportunity. Only a year before the Falkland

Island War began, amidst one of the worst economic recessions in generations, there was a transfer of power between military dictators. The military junta that had run the country since 1976 had fallen sorely out of favor, and in December of 1981, a new regime took over, this one headed by acting president, General Leopoldo Galtieri.

It was a member of Galtieri's recently installed cabinet, Admiral Jorge Anaya, that ultimately proved so instrumental in finding a military solution to what, for Argentines, was a long-standing problem of Falkland sovereignty. The nation was restive. Even with the regime change, the economy was terrible, with no signs of improvement. They were struggling badly with legitimacy, with being seen as a viable solution. In addition, there were a host of ongoing human rights violations hanging over the government, making their place in the international community tentative. Always being viewed as less than was taking its toll on morale. Taking the Falkland Islands back from the British Empire, one of the last bastions of colonialism, would be an effective way of restoring a sense of patriotic pride in the Argentine people, who had clung to the belief that the archipelago was rightfully theirs. It was Admiral Anaya that believed an invasion would work. He theorized that England would never defend her tiny island territory, half a globe away, with a definitive military force. The idea that the Brits would abdicate with ease wasn't without precedence; their own Secretary of Defense, John Nott, in that very year, had written it in a review of the situation in the South Atlantic. If the British weren't already unable to defend the Falklands, they very soon would be.

The national newspaper, La Presna, published an article in late 1981 with a simple plan. They believed that if United

Nations talks over the Islands were fruitless, direct action was necessary.

Cut off the supply line, they said.

Often a war flares out of what seems like a small action or seemingly meaningless gesture. When two tense nations are at odds, however, there is nothing small or meaningless in flying a flag on disputed ground.

As 1981 ended, United Nations talks around the Falkland Islands still had not materialized into a tangible solution. On March 19th, 1982, at the outset of the cold autumn season in the southern hemisphere, a band of Argentine scrap metal merchants brought their vessel close to South Georgia, an island strategically related to the Falklands. Eventually, those scrap metal merchants made landfall at Leith Harbor, and when they did, they flew their nation's flag high into the rippling breeze.

All that the British had on South Georgia was a small band of Marines and an Arctic Survey in the tiny settlement of Grytviken. Although the merchants were only much later revealed to be Argentine Marines, in disguise as civilian scientists, the damage had already been done. A civilian occupation of British territory had its humble beginnings. Humble, but the gesture had not gone unnoticed.

The Royal Navy gave the Argentines stern warnings. This act, however small and seemingly insignificant on the surface, would be interpreted as the first offensive action in the war. The Argentines, believing the warnings to be nothing but empty threats, held their ground. Within a few days of the flag flying, the Royal Navy command dispatched an ice breaker, the HMS Endurance, from Stanley to South Georgia.

The dominoes of war began to rapidly fall. The Royal Navy was surprised by the Argentine belligerence, the advances coming in spite of repeated warnings. With naval activity momentarily stunted in the South Atlantic, the Argentine junta decided its best move was to invade the islands, before we reinforced our fleet with additional ships.

On April 2nd, their army invaded the Falkland Islands. The following day, the Argentine army invaded South Georgia.

War had begun.

Chapter 3
Work Hard, Play Hard

We had all been given green berets, but we were still just boys. No one talked about the Falkland Islands; none of us quite understood the concept of a political pawn. As we prepared to deploy, no one knew anything about the United Nations.

As I've said, my unit was full of a bunch of tough guys. That's what the military amounts to, units of boys, all the toughest lads from their respective blocks. At the top of that rough and tumble heap is the green berets.

Training was rough, no doubt about it.

Marines are a tough lot that do a lot of hard drinking. I proved to be no different. Every night, my mates and I drank until we were pissed. Often, we didn't return until one of us had been in a bar or street brawl. Every weekend or leave, we went out drinking and trapping for ladies.

To say we were reckless may be right. Most of what mattered was how hard you fought and how well you trapped. They were a large part of gaining respect.

A military life breeds toughness. Soldiers are hardened through training, as well as while they're away from post. No one could back down from a fight, it simply wasn't how that was done. Whether or not the girl was a beauty, to turn her down was unconscionable. Survival and advancement of respect are relentless pursuits.

Being combat green is difficult on a soldier. My unit was split almost perfectly in two, the guys who had seen combat and those who had not.

A few guys in my unit were recently returned from deployment. Some had been to Northern Ireland, fighting the IRA street to street, house to house in some of the most complicated guerrilla and terrorist fighting in British military history. Others had been further away, fighting in campaigns in Asia, Europe, and Africa. A few were decorated and could boast of medals and a haughty stream of recognition.

Wherever they went, the experienced guys commanded immediate respect. No matter how hard you fought, or well you trapped, what kind of soldier you would be in a firefight could only be proven one way.

No one pined for warfare, but quietly, we all welcomed the opportunity to act.

When I went home to see Dad, the fight stayed with me. I'd go out for a few pints and end up battering some poor fella.

Chapter 4
The Trip That Never Was

It was 1982, the evening of March 23rd. It is a night that I will not forget. There are no pictures of it in my possession, but I wouldn't need them to remember anyway.

Everything is as clear as a bell.

We were in the South Atlantic Ocean. We were on our way south from the port in Montevideo. Upon leaving England, ending up in Uruguay wasn't on the agenda.

Our transport was an Arctic survey vessel, the John Biscoe. This certainly was not the customary means of getting around for Royal Marines, but nothing was moving forward in a customary manner. We had been ushered in secret out of the country.

Obviously, there was no time to wait.

I was on the back deck having a smoke, one of the rare moments I managed to steal away by myself. I remember that I was watching the sunset off the ship's starboard side when I heard a song come on the radio. Until the moment that song came on, I had been completely oblivious to the presence of music.

It's funny how a familiar song brings a distant moment into precise focus. Even now, my flesh goes cold and prickly just thinking back to it. Somewhere on board the John Biscoe, I heard, "Don't Let The Sun Go Down On Me" by Elton John.

No shit, I thought. No shit.

An old favorite song had suddenly been filled with new meaning.

How I ended up in Montevideo was among the stranger moments of my time in the Marines. Me standing on the deck of the John Biscoe, listening to Elton John's winsome classic, was the end of a surreal chain of events.

It all remains quite vivid to me, even now.

I had put in for a work assignment on the Falkland Islands earlier that winter. As luck would have it, I got what I had wished for.

A stretch on the South Atlantic seemed as good as any to spend a year of my enlistment. It was a secluded place, far away from any distractions.

I wanted to improve my skills and get into shape—the best condition of my life, I thought. I wanted to take up painting and learn how to operate a military motorcycle.

I also had my eye on saving a little money. With all the diversions back at home, saving money proved to be a bit challenging. No one in my family had ever gotten ahead of the game. A one-year detachment at the bottom of the world, away from any temptation to splurge, seemed like as good a place as any to sock away a few pounds.

As my mates and I prepared for our transfer, none of us knew about international tensions, or moves away from Colonialism. No one knew what was brewing between our government and the Argentineans. None of us knew a damn thing about crumbled talks at the United Nations, and none of us really had to. As the date for our departure crept ever nearer, all any one of us saw as challenging was the prospect of spending a year sequestered with the ugly mug next to us as company.

Marines are informed on a need to know basis. Apparently, according to our command, this was another instance in which we did not.

We all focused on the year to come, and more specifically, to the seven blissful days of shore leave that awaited us before starting our tour.

I shared the moment with forty-two other men. We were all aboard the same Royal Air Force flight, which was due south from Lyneham. I would wager that every single one of those guys remembers that day like it was yesterday. We were supposedly on our way to a promised shore leave in Brazil, where we eagerly anticipated a week of sun and drink and beautiful women; we never ended up touching down in Rio though.

Instead, our flight landed more than two thousand kilometers south, in Montevideo, Uruguay. Once we were on the ground, we were sequestered in the international airport. With everyone waiting in the terminal with orders to stay put, our commanding officer went off. He said that he needed to make a call on the telephone.

All of us were in disguise. I remember that we were posing as a football team on our way to a match. I remember thinking, a disguise? That's curious.

A bad feeling gnawing at the pit of my stomach in those uncertain moments soon followed. Most of the guys around me seemed to pass it off. They took it lightly, another droll military delay on the road to a well-deserved good time. A few of the guys jeered, hurry up and wait, as always. As the Boss hurried off and stayed away out of sight for an agonizingly long time, it became increasingly clear that there was something terribly wrong going on with our deployment.

Nothing added up—not the detour, not the disguise, and not the call, which seemed to go on for hours.

As the Boss came back around the corner, he shot all of us a look of unmistakable seriousness. We would not be turning back to Brazil.

On that call, he had received other orders.

There would be no shore leave, no drinking, and no shopping. As for those beautiful girls, they would have to go on another day living only in our dreams.

We didn't get back onto our plane. Instead, we were all rushed into a coach and taken down to the docks, where the John Biscoe awaited us. With nary more of an explanation than a change of plans, everyone got on.

Within an hour, we were at sea, on our way to the Falkland Islands. Something had indeed gone terribly wrong.

Some days later on, conjecture ran rampant among us. We were all still on the John Biscoe when we caught sight of a C130 passing low overhead.

I was on the deck with all of my mates now, and one of the rowdies turned and shouted out, "Let's shoot the moon."

We dropped our drawers. The military transport aircraft flew high in the sky and circled back for its second pass. As it drew closer to the water, buzzing the deck, the pilot and everyone on board got a view of our backsides, pointed straight up at the sky.

What a picture that this is going to make, I thought, laughing with all the others. We were a restless lot by then, just having a little fun. The C130 flew away, vanishing out of sight over the water, and not a single one of us gave a second thought about what we had just done. We went on talking and smoking and raising a little hell.

As it turns out though, that very moment became quite notorious. On the front page of the La Nacion, a Buenos Aires newspaper, the row full of our bare arses graced the cover, in full color too. We were the poster boys for British arrogance. Sure, there was a little madness in all of us, but what else were we to do? There was a growing anticipation, a fear of something coming; but for what, however, we had no idea.

Needless to say, my mates and I were grateful to finally see shore. Every single one of us got a sound bollicking for mooning that C130. No one gave a damn though—we had arrived. It was early on March 26 when we pulled into port in Stanley. We were in a new place, on the brink of war, and we laughed off our ration of shit.

Such is the life of a soldier. Penned up waiting, forced to take whatever was given, then given hell for pulling out a cadet's pratfall.

From the first moment I arrived, the Falkland Islands felt very small. The Marine barracks up in Moody Brook were dingy and hardly inviting. Brown carpet. Wooden walls. The bar was closed, but the smell of beer reeked from the stained furniture.

I wondered what I was getting myself into coming down here, for a year no less. No matter how I looked at this place, it hardly felt inviting.

We had been brought to the Falkland Islands urgently, but so far, we had not been told a single thing about why. I kept thinking that all of us were being treated like mushrooms—kept in the dark and fed shit. As Marines, we may be accustomed to operating on a need to know basis, but the constant feeling of not knowing took a gradual toll on us.

Most of us usually coped with the stresses of military life by blowing off with a few pints and throwing around a lot of tough talk, but the bar near the barracks appeared as though it never opened for business.

With no other word on what was to come next, I fell back on my goals. There would be my training, and I was determined to get into good shape.

Although the wind blew terribly stiff, I decided to go for a run that first day. Meanwhile, the other guys got their beds together and unpacked their things.

On that first run out from the barracks, a five-mile trot to get my wind up, I ended up making it to the edge of Stanley; I decided not to go into town though. The wind was blowing so hard in my face that my lungs were killing me. I was running at half my usual pace, my time for a routine run more than double what it normally was.

So much for my goal of getting in shape, I thought.

The next day, my muscles ached. I was in terrible pain. I had been as far north as Norway, above the Arctic Circle. This was cold though. On the afternoon of that second day though, word finally began to spread through our ranks. Major Norman had arrived at our barracks and began taking stock. Sections were given orders. Now aware that combat was imminent, the Marines all blacked out. The process of covering our faces with black paint was a shared ritual. Everything rubbed dark, nothing shiny for the enemy to see and shoot at.

We had been sent here early in order to relieve the old NP8901 detachment. They had been transferred north to South Georgia, in anticipation of Argentine aggressions.

Everyone was called into the bar in the barracks that was

now suddenly open, only we weren't tipping a pint, or trapping girls.

It was April 1st. Gaz and I took our place at a table and awaited Major Norman, who was scheduled to address the lot of us.

"Today you are going to die."

Gaz and I listened, rapt to every word.

"So go out there," Norman bellowed, "And do the job you are trained to do."

Only a few moments later, Gaz and I readied to receive our weapons. We were anxious, ready for this. We were moments away from transferring to tactical position.

"There's no such thing as a dead Marine," I said, taking my gun.

Gaz laughed out loud. "No point getting your head down now, is there?"

He was right.

Within minutes, we were on our way.

Chapter 5
The Cold, Wet Rock

On a map, the Falkland Islands don't appear to be particularly relevant. They are a small archipelago located in the South Atlantic, about three hundred miles east of the Patagonia region of Argentina, and just short of twenty-three hundred miles north of Antarctica. Altogether, there are seven hundred and seventy six tightly clustered islands, the bulk of the roughly 4,700 square kilometers in the two main masses, East and West Falkland.

The terrain is mostly rugged tundra. The hilly expanses are almost treeless, sprawling up to awe-inspiring mountain ranges, the peaks of which reach seven hundred snow dusted meters. A narrow body of water, the Falkland Sound, divides the two main islands, which in silhouette on a map oddly mirror one another against the pale blue sea. Flocks of penguins live along the rocky coastline, as do one of the last remaining albatross colonies on earth. Fish are abundant in the surrounding waters, and the concentrated population of seals has made the islands significant in the fur trade. Herds of reindeer roam free on the lush, grassy lowlands, with mountain goats up in the craggy peaks. In the terms of biodiversity, the Falkland Islands are included as part of the mild Antarctic zone, while to the eye, the local geography of the dense island group most closely resembles their neighbors to the west in Tierra Del Fuego.

To say the least, the weather on the Falkland Islands tends to be inhospitable to most dispositions. The conditions are prone to wild variations throughout any given day, through any season. There are often very blustery winds coming in hard from the west. Rainfall is heaviest in the spring and fall, but is common at any time of the year. It is not uncommon to see trace snowfall on the streets of Stanley, even in mid-summer.

A 2012 estimate of the entire archipelago's population was less than three thousand, largely homogenous people. They are considered Falkland Islanders. Most everyone that currently calls the Falkland Islands home is descended from either English, Scottish, or Welsh stock. There are a few citizens who can trace their heritage back to France, Spain, and Argentina, but those numbers are very few. Almost the entire island landscape is perfect for sheep grazing, which along with fishing, accounts for a large portion of the nation's gross domestic product. The CIA World Factbook lists the Falkland Islands as two hundred and twenty-first out of two hundred and twenty-nine in terms of the largest economies in the world.

That places its economy a whole thirty places back of Greenland.

While the Falkland Islands aren't idyllic, or particularly appealing as a destination for tourists, in terms of military strategy, it has become a point of vital importance.

Combined with the Georgian Islands east south east of the Falklands, the archipelago comprises one of the few useful outposts connecting England with the Antarctic, or with the southern edges of South America and Africa, of historic, national interest.

The South Atlantic isn't laid out quite like the South Pacific. The waters are not dotted with hundreds of islands suitable for a naval installment.

It is, in oceanic terms, a rather barren place.

Although some historians have speculated that there is ample evidence that the Fuegian people from nearby Patagonia visited the Falkland Islands during pre-historic times, the archipelago was uninhabited by humans when it was discovered by Europeans in the late 17th Century. British explorer John Strong sailed through the Falkland Sound in 1690 on his way to Chile, noting the lush country and prospects for a fishing trade, but he never made a claim; one was not stated until 1764 and 1766, when French and English expeditions made settlements on opposite islands. For a few years, they were independent of one another and remained mostly oblivious to the other's presence.

The first significant international attention turned toward the Falklands in 1770, when the "Falkland Crisis" brought two colonial powers to the brink of conflict. With competing claims on the discovery of the islands, the Spanish and English crowns engaged a diplomatic stand off and crept close enough to war that opposing armies and navies faced off on either side of the Falkland Sound. A few shots were fired and insults were shouted back and forth. There were rumbles in each nation's Parliament, but in the end, England and Spain arrived at a resolution; each nation decided, in a sense, to turn the other cheek and returned to their settlement.

There was a war for independence brewing in the American colony. Sovereignty of the islands would be fought for another day.

The British government eventually abandoned their colony on the Falklands in the late 18th Century. They left due to revised strategic considerations and the staggering cost of keeping such a remote outpost governed and supplied. The English flight left the area entirely to the Spanish, who used their fort there as a primitive prison camp and fishing outpost before they too abandoned the islands, leaving only a few stubborn gauchos and enterprising fishermen to try and carve a life out there.

Over the next century, control of the Falkland Islands was passed back and forth between nations. German merchants, Spanish explorers, and American prospectors all laid their claim, but eventually ceded their ambitions. Over the decades, Falkland waters gave their ports a reputation for being difficult to navigate. Many captains would only enter one under conditions of strict emergency, but they became a crucial stopover on trade ships rounding west toward Cape Horn in Tierra Del Fuego and east, to the Cape of Good Hope in Africa. A trading company was established, largely centering on the bustling local trade of fine wool and fish. In later years, the islands also became notable for shipwrecking and salvage, probably due in large part to the sheer number of damaged vessels that ended up in Stanley. During that period of time, the Argentine government took an interest in the Falklands, but they never rivaled existing claims. Then the Panama Canal was dug, giving American and European ships a faster route to the Pacific Ocean, and once again, Falkland significance waned tremendously.

As the 20th Century dawned, the Falkland Islands returned to prominence, this time with British interest in the yet untapped Antarctic region. The town of Stanley became a friendly stopover for teams of scientists and explorers on the way south.

During both World War I and II, the port on East Falkland played a role in staging for ships and planes. In December of 1914, the Battle of the Falkland Islands saw the Royal Air Force score a decisive victory over a German air squadron. In 1942, at the height of World War II, the British army sent a battalion of troops there on their way back from India, protecting against a Japanese invasion.

South American nationalism peaked post World War II. With success in the wool trade, and the desire for strategic military positioning, tensions simmering around Falkland Island sovereignty between Argentina and England came to a head again. In the 1960's, the United Nations passed a resolution on decolonization, a move that Argentine President Juan Peron viewed as friendly to his nation's interests there. The resolution gave colonial citizens the right to self-determination. It seemed as though the world was in tentative agreement that the Falklands belonged in Argentine hands, and Peron used this momentum to keep up the pressure for years. Finally, in 1965, another United Nations resolution passed, demanding that the two countries conduct joint negotiations in the interest of reaching a peaceful resolution on the islands sovereignty and thus, the wrangling began. The British contended steadfastly that sovereignty would be handed over only when the citizens approved of the measure. With tentative agreements seemingly in place, the Argentine military built an airfield east of Stanley.

Falkland Islanders never gave their consent though. This lack of a desire for change has remained central to the British claim for decades.

If the citizens don't want the change, they won't hand over control.

The Argentine government held to an opposite idea. They believed that they acquired the islands from Spain in 1816 as a part of their independence.

In this particular worldview, the English were illegal occupants of the islands, and had been since they first staked claim in 1833.

The tensions between Argentina and England never subsided. They only increased throughout the 1970s, with a last ditch effort to restore peaceful talks taking place early in the Thatcher reign; they never materialized.

In 1981, all talks in the British Parliament of turning control of the Falklands over to Argentina were abandoned.

The following spring, Argentina invaded the islands.

Chapter 6
Don't Break the Glass

We ran up the rear stairs of Government House, into the hallway. For the moment, we were safe from fire.

Everything was dark. For the first time in almost twenty-four hours, I lost track of Gaz. My disorientation was only momentary though. There were other voices in the house, speaking English, and I ran toward them. Amid those, I heard him. Over the smattering of gunfire going on outside the walls, the sound of a few friendly voices was comforting.

There was no time to debrief or recount our ordeal though. Section one raced through the house and up the stairs under orders from Sgt. Major Bill Muir.

"Upstairs, bedroom window," he shouted.

We took our orders without hesitation. I climbed the grand staircase to the second floor and raced down the long, carpeted hallway to get into position.

Gaz and I stormed into the first unoccupied bedroom we could find. I dropped onto all fours and crawled quickly toward the window.

Slowly, I parted the curtains. I pulled the thick fabric back just enough to get a bearing on what I was looking at and find my arc of fire.

The sky was still gray, but the sun was out, low in the sky.

There was a harsh, bright glare that was tough to see clearly through. When I situated myself right though, I could make out a decent view of the surrounding grounds. I had a clear shot on a few nearby alleys and roadways approaching the house.

I dropped my pack and situated my GPMG in the windowsill. It felt good to finally get it off of my back. Then, slowly, I pushed the barrel through the glass, shattering the pane, sending the shards outside onto the green slate roof below me.

"Don't smash the fucking windows," Sgt. Major Muir's voice came shouting from somewhere down the hallway.

I rolled my eyes as I cleared the pane with the long steel of my barrel. Gaz snickered to himself. Everyone throughout the house could hear his shout.

How the fuck can I fire through a window without breaking the glass? I thought. What the hell else am I supposed to do?

Then the wait part of hurry up and wait began.

The firefight had dwindled down. Outside, it became eerily quiet. Even though I had broken through the window, exposing myself to the blustery conditions, Government House remained warm, the heaters radiating welcome bursts of heat.

My head rested against the stock of the GPMC. The hard steel wasn't exactly the best pillow I had ever leaned on, but that didn't quite matter. I was beyond exhausted. A few times, I let my eyes droop closed and listened, drifting to catch a few winks, only to snap back and scan the spread before me. Nothing moved. The house was quiet.

Wrapped up into that false sense of security, I must have

nodded off to a harder, deeper sleep, because what woke me next was sudden and loud.

A burst of machine gun fire.

Shouts in English from rooms throughout Government House.

I heard thunderous footsteps and panicked screaming from the roof above me, muffled and unfamiliar.

Someone in the house clearly bellowed, "Argies on the roof!"

No matter how I repositioned the GPMC, I couldn't angle up toward the roof—someone could swing down from above. I pulled back some, giving myself enough room to fire back on anyone who may drop down in front of me.

The shouts persisted—volleys of gunfire echoed on all sides. Although I was uncertain who was shooting, I remained cool. I kept one eye on my gun, pointed outside—the other darted back to the hallway, where an invader could come running up at any second. The battle was closer now than it had been all morning.

Someone shouted, "Surrender, surrender."

There was a shuffle of footsteps and things got eerily quiet again. Only a few tension-riddled moments later, the three Argentine commandos that had dropped into the attic and caused the panic were being led away in custody. They were the first men captured by the British Marines all morning. Their seizure was a good sign, but only for a fleeting moment though. Word of our situation began to spread throughout the house.

Things outside were not looking good. We were badly outnumbered and had been outpositioned from the start.

Consequently, we were badly outgunned. As dour as our situation may have seemed though, we believed that we could hold out. That was the prevailing sentiment most of us clung to, even as we became more badly outnumbered on the ground. Six to one? That didn't seem too terribly bad.

From command's point of view though, holding out with no reinforcements to wait on arrival seemed like more of a fool's notion with each passing moment.

I remember that there was a clock in the room on a nightstand bedside. In those quiet, anxious moments, its persistent ticking reminded me that time was not actually standing still.

As those three Argentine prisoners were led away, I saw that it was just 8:30 in the morning. My first twenty-four hours in combat were coming to a close. Directly under our feet, on the main floor of Government House, an end to the battle itself was being actively pursued.

Multiple sections had already reported back to Major Norman in command, everyone's news sadly the same. The Boss had sorted through the reports and given Governor Hunt, still the island's leader, word of what the British army was up against. Armored vehicles had made land fall. They were rolling in toward Stanley as we sat waiting. There was little chance of our breaking through. No matter how we scrambled, how viciously we might have fought, we would not be regaining our foothold.

This may be a good time to negotiate.

Governor Hunt had already begun active discussions on an end to the hostilities. On the other end was Carlos Busser, a Vice Admiral in the Argentine Navy.

Hunt was a proud man, sometimes described as stubborn. He was an educated sort, full of that superiority. He had served in the Royal Air Force during World War II, after which he spent decades in diplomatic positions, most recently as a colonial administrator. To a man of Hunt's thinking and pedigree, the Falkland Islands were rightfully British territory; it was plain and simple. He was, quite naturally, reluctant to give in to any of the Argentine demands.

As Hunt hung on the phone, negotiating an end to the battle, he was doggedly determined of one thing. He was not going to surrender.

Although I heard none of the exchange, I remember hearing how Hunt managed to keep a stiff upper lip in refusal until Busser gave him a point on which he could not refuse. The Argentine Vice Admiral said that if the British did not lay down their weapons, they would start killing civilians.

By 9:30 in the morning, Gaz and I saw a group of five or six soldiers approaching out the window. As the party drew closer to Government House, I could see they were carrying a large, white flag. Like wildfire, a derisive tone filled the halls.

"I'm not surrendering to no spic bastards," one Marine announced.

Only instead of just shouting his derision though, he opened sniper fire on the vulnerable surrender party. Then all manner of panic broke out.

One of the Argentine soldiers dropped out of sight. I am not quite sure if he had been hit or ducked away, but those rogue shots sparked hostilities all over again.

The sniper was an old sweat. He'd seen his share of combat.

Over the years, he had done his share of killing. To his way of thinking, surrender wasn't an option.

It took half an hour to sort that out, but eventually, the flag went up again.

The imminent cessation of conflict brought new anxiety. New to war, now moments from perhaps becoming prisoners of war, none of us were sure what came next. One thing I was sure of, no one had told me to put down my gun yet. I did my best to shake off the calamity, calm my wracked nerves, and keep my gun trained.

A few moments later, Governor Hunt stepped proudly out of the front doors of Government House. On either side, a pair of Royal Marine officers flanked him. Awaiting him in the gravel below was Vice Admiral Busser, standing with a unit of ready Argentine soldiers. There were dozens, I thought. We'd be overrun in no time.

The two proud men met and regarded one another briefly.

"You have landed unlawfully on British territory," Hunt said, voice strong. "And I order you to remove yourself and your troops, forthwith."

Busser didn't budge. He didn't give the order to turn back. Instead, with a sharp eye, he ordered Hunt arrested and commanded his soldiers to take the building.

The soldiers ran up the front steps as Hunt and his Marine escorts were quietly led away. Sgt. Major Bill Muir shouted up the stairs, "Come on down, come on."

Then we heard the Argentine commandos break through the doors. Scattered shouts in Spanish filled the bottom floor as they ran up the stairs to secure the building.

The firefight was over. From that moment, I did what I was told. Gaz walked out first. I followed him down the corridor, down the staircase and out the front door.

I laid my gun down where I was told. I was scared shitless as I circled down into the courtyard, my hands thrust high up in the air.

Even though we were outnumbered and badly outgunned, the combat numbers were impressive. According to reports, there was somewhere close to six hundred Argentine soldiers lurking in the hills around Government House.

Less than a hundred British soldiers defended the island.

Every one of the soldiers that heard Major Mike Norman's talk the night before survived the firefight. Estimates said that we had managed to kill between twenty and thirty of their guys in the process.

When the Argentine Vice Admiral had come ashore to meet with the Governor, he was referred to as an unwanted guest. In their brief exchange though, Busser had informed Hunt of the cold, hard facts of the situation. The Argentines had almost three thousand men on-shore and another two thousand waiting for orders aboard their fleet. His threat to kill civilians wasn't an empty one; they could have slaughtered everyone.

Was this really happening? Just hours ago, we had been coarsely informed that we were to prepare ourselves for duty and death, in that order. Not a single one of us could have guessed that our morning would have ended in the posture of surrender.

You can still find the picture of what came after Hunt gave the surrender order, with those Argentine soldiers storming into Government House. It's not too difficult at all, actually. You can call it up in an online search, and it's among the first to pop up. You can find it in every single history book about the Falkland Island War.

We were marched down the stairs. In single file, we passed through the foyer and out of the house. One by one, our weapons were taken from us. We were searched by a small group of Argentine Special Forces. There were maybe twenty of them in the courtyard, no more, machine guns out, grenades hanging off of their belts.

They shouted at us, barking out orders, but few of us spoke any Spanish. We could hardly understand what they were saying, but we clearly understood the scope of the situation. When the house was empty of Royal Marines, we were told to lay face down in the road, hands up above our heads, and feet out.

Although I did not hear him, somewhere in the group of people preparing to deal with us, a photographer began snapping our picture.

Within hours of that battlefield photographer snapping that picture, the black and white image spread around the world. This was big news.

What the picture meant needed no interpretation. A failed set of United Nations talks had led to war, and the Argentine army had beaten the British Marines in the first battle. Forget about the number of invaders and the element of surprise; forget that not a single British lad died in losing. The circumstances hardly seemed to matter.

The Crown had been compromised.

Even though the word of war spread at a snail's pace in 1982 compared to what it does now, it still did not take long to reach the opposing governments. The image of a dozen British Royal Marines, face down on the rock road with Argentine soldiers prowling up their backs, machine guns pointed, got blood boiling throughout the United Kingdom. Everything else would go on immediate hold while a response was sorted out.

I'm in that picture. I'm the lad, second nearest to front and center. My head is down as ordered, toes ground into the rocks. When I look at it, I still think I look pretty damn good, my Green Beret on straight.

Even more curious for me to think back now is that in the halls of power, someone saw me. My fifteen minutes of fame spent in a prone, helpless position that would ultimately serve as a saber rattling call to war.

At least I'm grateful for my ordered appearance.

When I reflect on that morning now, so much of what I do not remember comes across a little clearer. A few of the guys look like they're craning for a look, hopeful of an opportunity to fight back. I remember that I was deathly afraid of what came next.

I was still wet behind the ears. I wasn't an old sweat yet. I did not speak a single word of Spanish. All that I remember was the click of boot heels, the sounds of uncertain chatter and the clangs of metal against metal as our weapons piled outside.

I did not see the guns pointed at me. I knew they were there by sound though and as our arrogant captors humiliated us, I remember having another fleeting thought. They are not going to kill us. We are all going to make it through this.

Word of Argentine victory reached South America.

Later that day, on a Friday afternoon in Buenos Aires, a celebratory crowd began to form in the streets. Eventually, over two hundred thousand happy Argentines filled into the old Plaza de Mayo. They flew the light blue and white flags and banners, relishing in the liberation of what was locally called Islas Malvinas.

Back home in England, an overwhelming storm of public opinion had already formed and was brewing out of control.

And the rest of the world waited with baited breath for the British response.

PART II: An Old Sweat

Chapter 7
"Wideawake"

The notion of becoming a "prisoner of war" arrives on one with a dubious sense.

We have all seen the movies. We've internalized images of war-ragged soldiers shivering in a bitter cold, beaten and taunted and sorely underfed by their captors.

Every soldier has seen and pondered over this dilemma as well. It is a far better fate to die with your boots on than to linger helplessly as a captive.

All of the lads in Section One were past that fear for our lives, but we were not far enough into the clear to be comfortable.

A hundred thoughts raced through my head like loose threads unraveling all at once. Most of them fell under some category of, what the fuck is going on? When I look at those pictures of myself, hands up, face smeared with black paint, that's what's going through my head.

What the fuck is going on?

Quite a number of decades had passed since the British army had encountered the dilemma of having prisoners of war—what to do and how to negotiate their release. It hadn't been since the Second World War, when the POWs numbered in the thousands, that the question had been asked. Our defeat at Government House in Stanley presented Prime Minster Thatcher, and her cabinet, a whole new set of diplomatic problems.

Marine training doesn't tell you precisely what to do when captured, but the implication should be very clear. Maintain a strong stance, put up a wall of defiance. Do not say a word. Don't give the sodden enemy anything to use against you.

Looking back at that hand full of pictures from our capture that morning, you can see the cool bravado in our eyes, our ready postures.

What the fuck? You're not getting anything out of me.

After we were all sorted and ordered like heads of cattle, the lads from Section One got into a transport vehicle. We were escorted by a small group of Argentine commandos, the same soldiers we'd fired on throughout the morning. The hour was dragging on toward the afternoon, and the panic of what would happen to us as newly captured prisoners of war was wearing thinner with each moment.

Although these underfed bastards were strutting around and posing for celebratory pictures, they were as scared as we were—probably more so. They're not going to line us up and shoot us, I thought. We aren't going to be humiliated or made an example of; that had already happened in the moment that we threw our hands up. By now, our shell-shocked mugs had been broadcast to the world. The worst was over with.

What would be coming next, however, remained curiously up in the air.

An eerie calm came spread over us as we lined up in an orderly fashion and sat down quietly on the lawn. As we eventually boarded our transport, not one of the Marines had much to say. All the faces were there, Gaz and Bernie and Eggman. We exchanged a few sideways glances, darting eyes between familiar faces. What we managed to convey in that silence was a well-heeled sense of skepticism at best.

We sat around for quite a long time while the Argentine commandoes waited on their orders. As I watched them operate, I realized that they were worried. Perhaps they hadn't expected to rout us as they had? Finally, the vehicle engine started and we circled down out of the Government House lot. We recognized that we were being driven back up toward Moody Brook, and the barracks that had been destroyed earlier in the day, by Argentine grenades and a fierce volley of gunfire.

A lazy plume of smoke drifted up on the breeze as we approached. The series of devastated buildings, which were still smoldering, proved to be a sobering reminder. Had any one of us been moved from those barracks even an hour later, our bodies would be riddled with holes, just like the barrack walls. Our lives had been saved by a narrow margin.

When we arrived at Moody Brook proper, we were dispatched from the transport. We were ordered to pick up whatever of our personal affects we could find in the rubble, as well as any kit we wanted, before getting back on. None of us had been posted in these barracks very long; three days is not enough to call a place your home.

The somber mood turned even further down as we rummaged. I didn't manage to find much, as only a few things of mine had survived. Some of the others lads walked away with disappointment, but not me.

Something told me it was unwise to delve into the wreckage with much hope.

An hour or so later, we pulled away from Moody Brook. As the barracks vanished in the rear view, an autumn sun was already hanging low in the western sky.

The transport turned down the road in the direction of the Stanley airport. What would come next for us became quite clear.

We were about to be escorted off of the Falklands.

One of the Argentine soldiers piped up, bravely breaking the icy silence. "Do you think you'll be back here?" he asked.

I bristled at the sound of his voice, his words of broken English. Every one of the Marines in Section One would have answered him similarly had we drummed up enough nerve to speak our minds in that moment.

Only one of us did though.

"Sure as hell we will be back," one Marine replied.

His salty toned response brought an ashen expression to the quizzical Argentine commando's face. The rest of us simpered in agreement.

Sure as hell we will, I thought. No one's gonna to take this lying down.

Had that bold Marine given the commandos anything by vocalizing defiance? Could he take that back to his commander and use it against us?

Who knows? All that I can say, looking back on that moment now, is that it felt good to hear him say that we'd be back—pretty damn good, actually.

A lot can change in a short time. Although the rest of the

ride out, through the town of Stanley to the airport, only took a few moments, a critical shift had occurred.

I felt as though we were already gaining back the upper hand on these guys, who so wrongly believed that the Royal Marines would all simply crawl back to London with our tails limp between our legs. That commando needed to be aware. He needed a lesson in the simple fact that the Crown does not whimper when stricken; she roars.

We were ordered off the transport on the shell battered airfield. A deafening wind confronted us as, once again, we were lined up and sorted out. A plane awaited us and we boarded, like school children on a trip, in single file.

We had already been ordered to surrender our weapons. Now lined up and awaiting orders to get on the plane, we were given a full body search. I remember one of the lads had a six-inch knife hidden in his boot. When the Argentinean commando found it and held out the steel blade, we all got a pretty good laugh.

The look on his face though? Pure panic. What was that Marine's intent? Was he going to run every commando through while in mid-air?

On board, we looked around the cabin as we took our seats. Although uncomfortable, a comforting sense of familiarity came over me. We were being combined with a few lads from the other sections. The battle smoke had hardly been extinguished, but NP8901 was already reforming yet.

I heard the plane propellers sputter to a start. I took a deep breath as we backed slowly up along the runway, held for a moment, and then sped out toward the dusk gray horizon, now reduced to a jagged outline.

Then the wheels lifted. I craned my head to watch as

everything on the ground below got smaller and eventually disappeared.

We were in the air, the Falkland Islands growing smaller with each second.

The plane ride took us on a northwest route across the Atlantic Ocean. Similar understandings dawned on each of us: everything seemed to be fine, aside from our surrender, which was feeling more and more like a small diversion.

As we flattened out at cruising altitude, a bit of laughter played amongst a few of the lads. The old sweats cracked jokes. A few of the guys had been brimming with stories, boasting loudly about what had happened during the morning firefight.

I joined in. The way I saw it, there was no use in missing out on all of the fun. I told the story of my bollicking for breaking the bedroom window glass with my gun. The tale got a few nods from the lads and more than a few laughs.

On that day, I was no longer green. I had become an old sweat too.

Those questions of how I would respond under fire were a thing of the past. What had started out that morning as an uncertainty had been solidified on that plane ride.

Survivor of a firefight, I was not only a soldier. I had become a Royal Marine.

Under a pitch-black sky, our C130 aircraft began a gradual descent. I looked out the windows to see that we were approaching an airport with a smattering of surface lights. The plane touched down at Comodoro Rivadavia, a base in southern Argentina.

Once on the ground, a squadron of Argentinean commandos surrounded us. Their guns were pointed as we were shuffled between planes, this time to a civilian aircraft.

Although no one knew where, at least we were taking off over land. At the front of the plane, Rex Hunt and his wife took their seats.

We eventually touched back down in Uruguay. Only a few days before, NP8901 had passed through the same Montevideo airport—now that seemed like a lifetime ago. Unlike at Comodoro Rivadavia, there was no unit of Argentinean commandos, with their guns trained on us. Ushered off of the plane like civilians, we were transported by a normal city bus out of the airport complex, escorted only by police.

I was scared shitless, but a sense of skepticism had crept in and taken over. Where were we being taken? A military camp? A prison? The only unfamiliar face aboard that bus was the driver, who steered us through the night. I knocked off a few times, only to startle and look out, unable to see more than the roadside around us.

Only a short distance down the highway, the lights of civilization reappeared on the horizon. Everyone craned eagerly as what appeared to be a hotel emerged ahead.

We pulled off of the highway into an empty parking lot, where the police vehicles lined up and stopped. The officers got out and prepared to move us.

Everyone shot a look around, wondering what was going on. This can't really be happening, can it? What are we doing at a damn hotel?

We were escorted off of the transports and into the evening air. The lack of a bitter, stiff wind in my face felt good. In spite of uncertainty, the air was refreshing.

None of the lads came from a life of luxury—that was for Generals and Admirals. In spite of our unfamiliarity with the finer things, we sure knew what they looked like when we saw them. The hotel we had been brought to was a four-star affair.

I can still recall the outline of dim moonlight on the beach, spread as far in either direction as my eye could see. The view was unforgettable. It was the kind of thing that a young, Yorkshire born lad can only dream of until he sees it for himself.

One by one, we trudged in through the hotel's grand entry-way. We must have been quite a sight for the crew on duty that night, a ragged string of British Marines, filthy from head to toe and streaked in black camouflage, passing through the once quiet lobby.

First, we were shown to our beds, two to a room. My assigned bunkmate was Danny, and as we walked around the room, jaws on the floor, everything still seemed strange to us.

"Check it out," Danny shouted, from the bathroom.

I took a look inside as he marveled like an ape over the bidet styled toilet. "Look at this," he went on. "It's got something to wash your feet in."

"Bollocks," I replied.

A room was a room. By now, I was bloody hungry. I can still remember the ocean outside and the parking lot around the hall, crawling with police lights.

What the hell is going on?

Around midnight, we were all ushered back downstairs and show into a banquet room, where a food spread awaited us. There were thick cuts of steak, cooked vegetables, and hunks of bread and butter. The sight of it nearly brought me to my knees with joy.

Suddenly, that dark, skeptical cloud broke free of its mooring. An overjoyed feeling coursed through all of us, seemingly at once. Every Marine in that room was ravenous, our last solid meal long since forgotten, and every single one of us would have knocked down a wall for a sip of ale, cold or otherwise. Too many days had passed us by, and we cheered lustily as the first tray of beers went out on the trolley, even if it was beer mixed with soft drinks. The next tray was nothing but booze.

We found our places at the table, assigned by rank. Hungers were satisfied and thirsts slaked. A merry air filled the room as we drank, ate, and laughed. The trays of beer kept coming, one after another. We felt like bridegrooms or returning heroes.

I can't remember a pint that tasted quite so good. My nerves cooled gradually with each slurp of suds. I would hazard a guess that the rest of the lads in NP8901 probably look back on those rounds of drinks the same way. We were all battered beyond exhaustion, but looking back, that was one of the best damn meals of my life. We all drank as long into the night as they allowed us to.

Another, much quieter, sense arose as we all staggered drunkenly to the lifts and fell back to our rooms, where we would sleep in a proper bed for the first time in days. The feast was luxurious, but it made for a surreal scene.

Something wasn't quite adding up.

A four star, beach front hotel, a lavish spread of beer and food, a bed that would make any of the bunk sleeping lads back home jealous—these were not the images anyone carried for prisoners of war.

And if we weren't POWs, what were we?

While the lads and I feasted and slept around the hotel that night, the greater response from the British government was well underway.

On Monday, April 5th, roughly seventy-two hours after Government House fell to the squads of Argentine commandos, the HMS Invincible set sail out of Portsmouth. She regaled in patriotic glory, cutting through the chop with the Hermes along her side. The pictures were broadcast wide across the Empire and are quite staggering to behold. The massive ship, with flags unfurled, set against the morning sun. Sailing during spring in the Northern Hemisphere, she was escorted by a crowd of happy onlookers, people waving from yacht decks and fishing boats while passing through the narrow channel, under the shadow of Southsea Castle, out of harbor. Their departure was a clear sign of force.

A light aircraft carrier and the lead ship in the Royal Navy's fleet, the Invincible stood as immediate proof that the British government would not take the Argentine attempt to seize control of the Falkland Islands as a light incursion. The Junta had wagered that a forceful response from the Crown halfway across the world would be too far-flung and too expensive; they were entirely off base. The intent behind the aggressive launch of the HMS Invincible was twofold; on one hand, it was meant to embolden the restless people at home, and on the other, to serve as a warning to those still celebrating victory in the streets of Buenos Aires. British force would weigh in on the resolution, one way or another. Perhaps they should consider those gains short-lived.

The diplomatic solution to conflict became a work in progress from the moment Governor Rex Hunt stepped off of the porch and surrendered control of the islands. Throughout March and into April, the Argentine Junta had been clinging to a faint hope that the Americans, with whom they had built up some positive diplomatic relations, would back their anti-colonial actions; they found, almost immediately, that this hope would prove to be misguided. 1982 was in the dead of the Cold War, and American backing was never a realistic possibility, not in defiance of an old, trusted ally. American Secretary of Defense Casper Weinberger was bullish on backing British actions in the Falklands, just so long as they were not caught doing so.

While British foreign secretary Francis Pym, along with his old friend, US Secretary of State Alexander Haig, worked round the clock to address the needs of both nations, Prime Minister Thatcher had other concerns. The woman who would become known as "the Iron Lady," for a multitude of conflicting reasons, not all of them affectionate, was more in line with the British people. As a whole, the man on the London streets hardly seemed interested in anything like a diplomatic solution. A hostile act on sovereign British territory was to be met with a strong show of force. Thatcher's thirst for conflict proved to be an unrelenting tide.

Ships from Portsmouth were cause for celebration. An early look at the polls, both culled formally and from bar stools city to country, showed that public opinion was squarely with taking the islands back. The people would stand for nothing less than full sovereignty being restored in the Falkland Islands. The global move away from colonialism had come with more than its share of pratfalls for the Empire. Prime Minister Thatcher was not so secretly determined to avoid making the same mistakes that her predecessors had made as recently as thirty years earlier, when, in the 1950's, handing over the Suez Canal to the Egyptians turned into a debacle on the world stage.

Instead of holding back her cards, Thatcher hastily set up a multi-disciplinary committee and dubbed it "The War Cabinet." Through that vehicle, she set about resolving the Falkland conflict. The initial thrust by Thatcher's hand-picked Cabinet was to frame the Argentines as aggressors in world opinion. She was careful to place warmongers in the Junta as squarely in the wrong for the invasion. The Argentine response to this public relations move proved clumsy. Relatively inexperienced in dealing with international incidents on such a scale, aside from squabbles with their South American neighbors, the Junta was caught on their heels and unable to coordinate a compelling counter point. The following afternoon, British ambassador to the United Nations, Sir Anthony Parsons, engineered the passage of Resolution 502, which stressed the need for an immediate Argentine withdrawal and chastised the use of force as illegitimate. France followed, agreeing to a temporary halt to their export of aircraft and missiles to the Argentines. Consequently, the Junta's military capabilities were cut off at the knee. Less than a week after the invasion, a one-month international trade embargo was secured against Argentina, with an option granted for extension for as long as was necessary to work out a solution.

A noose had been placed around the Junta's neck. As the Invincible and Hermes set sail on the Atlantic Ocean, that rope only grew tighter with each passing hour.

Over the weeks to follow, the number of ships that departed from British ports around the world was nothing short of staggering. Each vessel was destined for a meet up in the South Atlantic Ocean. Hulking battleships, a host of destroyers, aircraft carriers, decks lined with fighter jets—all ready to swarm. Every one of those ships set sail on what would be a nine thousand mile trip into the heart of a growing war zone.

A menacing task force, such as the one that was mounting against the Argentines, requires a place to stage its operation. A chain of command the length of the Atlantic Ocean would fall apart, immediately. In the lead up to the Falkland Conflict, that critical line was established off of the west coast of Ascension Island, near the main town of Georgetown. Located approximately half way between England and the Falkland Islands, a few hundred clicks south of the Equator, the isolated volcanic archipelago proved a vital aspect in the chain of command, and access to its wartime lease came courtesy of the Americans.

American support could not come in the form of supplies or money, nor could the Yankees come in and fight on the ground. While the nostalgic image of British and Yankee soldiers fighting an enemy side by side, like they did in World War II, would swell confidence back at home, it would not cooperate with Weinberger's stated need. The Americans wanted discretion. Rather, support came in the form of logistics.

A generation earlier, during the Second World War, American forces had constructed a state of the art military airfield in the black lava flow of Ascension Island. The airfield was called Wideawake. Once home to the world's longest runway, the barren island became a key strategic vantage point, one where the British military could dig in their heels. As the first few hectic days after the surrender at Government House waned and hostilities temporarily abated, both nations worked out an agreement for access. Once American President Ronald Reagan and Prime Minster Thatcher worked out the politics of refueling Royal Air Force jets, British oil tankers were anchored. The signal was given. Vulcan bombers would deploy on sortie and patrol from Wide Awake.

The rate of military activity ramped up. Within a week, it peaked around four hundred movements each day. A remote air base if ever there was one, Wide Awake went from one of the most obscure in the world to the busiest, practically overnight.

British muscle was flexing, and every move was carefully calculated to relay an air of seriousness to the heads of state across the sea in Buenos Aires.

At breakfast in the hotel lobby the next morning, we walked into a manic scene. If there were any civilians around, I don't remember. Everyone wanted to know what happened to Jim's section, the last unaccounted for back in the Falklands.

The hotel staff asked our group to sign off on all the beer we had drank the night before. The party was over and the check had come painfully due. Bollocks, we thought through our searing hangovers. We all had a good laugh and looked around as though someone in the crew had gone mad. Who did we belong to? No one knew who exactly was supposed to foot the bill here.

I don't know which Marine was responsible for it, but I remember hearing that someone wrote on one of those receipts:

"Thatcher, SV Boot."

The message? Send it back to the United Kingdom.

It was early on a Saturday morning. We were still only twenty-four hours past our capture back at Government House. Stories of chaos went around between the bored Marines as they passed away the tedious hours after breakfast.

The picture became clearer as more information came in. We learned that Jim's section had been thrown into an Argentine prison; clearly they did not get the steak and beer, two lads to a luxury room treatment. They ended up taking shelter in a secluded shepherd's hut, owned by a woman named Mrs. Watson, and staying hidden there for many hours without access to a radio. They had been worried about the size of Argentine forces over civilian deaths—no one told them that both the Royal Marines and the Islander population had gotten off without casualties. Eventually, they used a civilian radio to call in their surrender to the Argentines, only after their reluctant commanding officer ordered their weapons destroyed and buried in the yard outside.

Our humor was back. No one was quite sure what we should do when we saw the captured section again, razz or rally behind them. Our grit and resolve slowly returned as well. Control of the situation had come back together—it seemed as though defeat in battle, and eventual capture, would prove mere diversions on the road. By early afternoon, a squadron of Marines left on a VC-10 airliner. They were headed back to Montevideo, where they would pick up Governor Rex Hunt; we also heard that the rest of NP8901 would be accompanying the Governor on his trip back home as well.

Anyone whose morale may have flagged was surely rousing back to form.

The following Monday morning, April 5th, was quite warm, over eighty degrees Fahrenheit. Summer weather had arrived early in England.

Section One was due to arrive back at Brize Norton, an RAF base in Oxfordshire, a few miles northwest of London. A few of the other sections from the firefight were on that inbound flight with us, and no one knew what to expect as far as a welcome.

I was included in that lot of returning Marines. To say that I was fearful of what would meet me at home would be a gross exaggeration. I think my state of mind was typical for the others gripping their seats. As we began our descent toward the airfield and saw the crowd massed, I hung on uncertainly. We certainly had all gotten our fifteen minutes; my lingering anxiety was that our fame had been gotten in disgrace.

Turns out, I was wrong in my thinking. We had not done the Crown any disservice. As the men of NC8901 stepped off of the plane, onto the Brize Norton airstrip, the welcome we got proved to be quite glorious. It was one befitting a group of returning heroes; no one waving and cheering saw us as goats.

Perhaps they all knew what command was in store for us.

At the center of our welcome party was Sir Stuart Robert Pringle, a Commandant General of the Royal Marines. Everyone knew Pringle, or had at least heard his story. Pringle had joined the Marines in the year after World War II ended and quickly rose to become something of a titanic figure in the 45 Commando. Only six months before the Falkland conflict, in October 1981, Pringle had been severely wounded, losing his leg in an IRA bombing of his car outside of his Dulwich, South London home. He was lucky to be alive. The story famously goes that he was headed out for a run with his dog, Bella, and, on regaining his composure, asked his rescuer bravely, "How is my dog?"

An attendant brought Pringle out onto the stage in his wheelchair, where he bravely prepared to deliver an address. All the lads in NC8901 stood in awe of the wounded hero, but when the moment came for our greeting, Pringle did us an unexpected turn. The dignified man stood out of his chair and beamed out upon us.

Hearts in the crowd stopped in awe.

Pringle wanted to personally shake each of our hands. Looking him in the eye, taking his still rugged grip in mine, was one of the proudest moments of my life. For that brief moment, the deafening roar washed away, and it was only the two of us.

When we finally settled in to listen to his speech, Pringle spoke in a voice both clear and true. Then the wounded man performed what felt like his second miraculous turn as Commandant General on that day.

He told all of us that we would be going back. As that truth sank in, each one of us was filled with a pride we had never experienced before.

We would be a vital part of a task force that, as we soon learned, was already in the process of mobilizing in the South Atlantic.

Our moment of infamy would soon be redeemed. We would take back the Falkland Islands.

Chapter 8
The Armpit of Luxury

Once back in Britain, we all got a couple of weeks of leave before we were supposed to ship out again. Leave is never a bad thing. For most of us, though, I think this time, it was also a bittersweet reality.

Most of us were still amped up from the firefight; I know that I was. That's not the kind of adrenaline that wears off overnight. We had gotten a hero's welcome, a little pomp and circumstance. Stepping away proved a comedown, by comparison. We packed our bags with whatever we needed, boarded buses and trains, and then went our separate ways, back to see our families.

During that first week back in England, I went home to my dad's house. We were supposed to take a few days to get some rest and relaxation, to charge the batteries. What it turned out to be for me was one bloody drunken binge.

Maybe I was pumped up, still a bit full of myself when I walked into his house. I don't quite remember walking from the station or heading up the path. What is burned clear in my memory is Dad's response to my mug coming through the doorway, however.

"Where the hell have you been?"

I bucked up. I had taken more than my share of his shit over the years. Besides, I was a man now. I looked Dad square in the eye and calmly replied, "The Falklands."

"Where the hell is that?"

He groused a bit as I explained. I told him where I had been, about the firefight, and how we had ultimately surrendered to the Argentineans at Government House.

"Well," he replied. "I could have done a better job than that."

That was all I got from the old man. He didn't have much more to offer than to slag his son off for what he saw as a shame. Dad spurned me and turned away.

Could he have done better? I don't know, but his words, cruel and ill timed, knocked me for a loop.

In hindsight, I don't know quite what I expected from the old sourpuss. Maybe deep down, I knew he wasn't quite capable of offering me solace, or even a decent word.

Perhaps I knew he would compare us, giving me a dig in the process. Still, in those days following my return, I spun out a bit. I was set to bunk in his house, but instead I ended up spending every moment I could down at one of the local pubs drinking, telling war stories and, after nightfall, trapping. Word had gotten around about the lads in the Falklands and being one of them gave me the real hero's welcome I was hungry for. Everyone wanted to hear a tale or two and to share a pint, and women wanted to share their beds with a warrior. They saw me as a tough guy, and I didn't mind playing up the part of the bloke who had seen the shit and lived to tell the story.

Most of those nights back at home, I was out with strangers and trapping a few women I had never seen before or would see again.

Better a stranger than Dad, I thought.

Being home on leave was daunting, more than because of Dad's cold shoulder. It's the space between that can be the toughest to endure. Before I even walked through Dad's door, I was ready to get back to the adventure.

On one of those afternoons back home, I managed to catch up with Mom and my sister. Everything was a drunken blur, but I remember ringing them up one day and they agreed to come out. No one wanted to spend any more time with Dad than we had to, so we made a plan. We decided to meet down at the pub to have lunch and a pint.

Mom was proud of me; this much I could count on. She had kept all of the news clippings of my time in the service. They caught me up on their lives and listened to my stories. Then she gave me a warm embrace after we ate, after which, we parted calmly.

When it was time to go back to base, there was no big good-bye, no production. Dad had already estranged himself from me. We were cordial, but I walked out of his house the same way that I walked in. We parted without ceremony.

As I got back on the road to meet up with my section, I thought, what a bloody waste of time going back home is.

Once back, I began to feel more at home as we prepared for our return. Each of us got new gear. We were fitted for a new kit that we'd take down to the Falklands.

We had become quite a tight-knit group; looking back, I think everyone felt that time away from each other was a tough slog. The lads in my section, more than Dad and even my Mom, had become my family now. Being away from them was tough. When I walked back in and saw their faces, I was happier than I'd been in a long time.

We had become notable figures around the base and in town, and we quite enjoyed our brief time as minor celebrities. We did a lot of strutting around the halls and barracks. Only roughly one-third of the Royal Marines were being sent to the South Atlantic, meaning quite a few of our mates were jealous being stuck at home. We had seen the shit and were getting the chance to go back and prove ourselves a second time.

I felt like a big man. To hell with what Dad had to say, I thought.

When we went out for a drink or two, which was every night, we stood tall. Our chests thrust out as we bragged and boasted of our exploits.

I remember one night standing outside of a wine bar. We were all queued up, waiting to get inside. Maybe it was the night before we were scheduled to leave, I don't recall, but what remains burned into my brain is how the woman in line gave us a hard time.

Maybe we had gone overboard. Maybe our boasting about the Falklands, and this and that, was untoward, but she gave us a pretty good bollicking.

"Why the hell aren't you down there, fighting with the rest?" she shouted.

All of us shut our mouths and let her have her that moment. Maybe we should have been playing the part of Marines with more dignity.

Maybe she was right, hell, I don't know. I do know that we all were keenly aware that regardless of her opinion, we would be up to our necks in shit soon enough.

After enduring those long couple of weeks back home, we were all flown down to Ascension Island on board a

DC-10, a military plane. The lads of NP8901 had been the first detachment into the Falkland Islands. Now we had to catch up.

We landed on Ascension Island in the midst of the already assembled task force. As I stepped off of that plane, I was treated to the most impressive view I had ever seen. The weather was tropical, the warmth was inviting as it caressed your face. The calm sea surrounding our position was alive with activity: massive war ships as far as the eye could see, a fleet of fighter-lined carriers, battleships, and destroyers.

The show of force was a magnificent sight. It was breathtaking, and as I think back on it now, all that muscle made me proud.

We were ordered to bunk in an old villa that was situated on top of a steep mountain. Once again, I felt as though we were treated better than ordinary grunts. There were swimming pools, warm breezes, and beautiful views of the island and sea. Throughout the day and night, helicopters circled overhead, moving personnel here and there.

Dad may have clung to the belief that he could have done better, but he never took a vacation like this one.

I was full up though, back in my element, military adventure resumed.

We only spent three days on Ascension Island, but those few days remain burned in the nicer moments of my memory. We trained religiously. We worked with weapons, taking a thousand shots of target practice with high-powered sniper rifles. We swam in the villa pools and on the beaches. We ran up and down the steep volcanic slopes, pushing harder to get stronger, faster. On top of Green Mountain was an old Marine barracks, built out of solid granite. It had been in place since the first Royal Marines were stationed there centuries before.

One afternoon, the lads of NP8901 ran up the side of the nearly nine hundred-meter peak, through lava fields and intense heat, only to marvel at its massive size. As I caught my breath, I remember thinking that the barracks was a remarkable feat of engineering. Looking back down the way we'd come up, the sheer effort and manpower required to move such colossal stones up from the shores was inspiring.

A few bizarre events transpired over those few days, no surprise there. We had been given caution by our command to steer clear of what they called "sea piranhas," a vicious little carnivorous fish that would swarm and chop you to bits with lines of razor sharp teeth. We scoffed a bit at the idea. We were accustomed to finding humor in everything, that is, until the first casualty of the Falkland Island War fell to a fish rather than an Argentinean rifle. Some poor lad was chopped to bloody shreds.

I'd hate to hear what his old man would have to say for his fate.

During those early days of our return, I believe that someone was looking out for us. We were, at every turn, treated differently than the rest.

NP8901 had still not been designated as part of a proper command. Major Mike Norman was still doling out orders as our leader, but we were adrift, awaiting further assignment. Our brief stay on Ascension Island felt a little bit like recreation, and however strange that might have been, none of us would be heard complaining.

I can still picture us on a mountaintop villa, sunning our

bodies. We were full of the idea that we were war heroes, strutting around like we were cocks of the walk.

Then came the time for the Task Force to depart.

The English have a rich history with being creative in defense of their native island. Sometimes a proper ship simply is not available when needed.

At the Battle of Dunkirk, during the fevered peak of World War II, with docks damaged and the Allied fleet and armies battered by waves of German bombers, thousands of troops were evacuated across the English Channel under a heavy fog in anything seaworthy, from fishing boats to bathtubs. That rescue operation didn't just preserve the lives of those soldiers to fight another day; that effort may well have turned the tide of the entire war. Might without creativity leaves too much to chance. Ingenuity may not be the father of victory, but it has often sired a great deal of hope.

The British military was caught without a contingency plan for the Falkland invasion as it had occurred; the task force had to be hastily assembled if the Crown was going to offer the quick, decisive response it desired. On the forth of April, the nuclear submarine, Conqueror, set sail from port in France. The next morning a pair of aircraft carriers, Invincible and the flagship HMS Hermes, departed from Portsmouth, the latter of which was featured on the cover of Newsweek only a few days later under the headline, "The Empire Strikes Back." The aircraft carriers, with their escorts alongside, ferried a great many of the soldiers that would comprise the ground attack to re-take the Islands.

In the fleet that set sail from Ascension Island was an ocean liner, a breathtaking vessel that, aside from entertaining its share of retired generals, came with no notable military pedigree. Called out of the middle of a recreational cruise in the Mediterranean Sea on April 3rd, the SS Canberra was delivered into a British port, where it was transformed from a top of the line luxury liner to troop carrier, practically overnight. Only a week after the firefight, on the ninth of April, her Captain, Dennis Scott-Masson, departed south toward the Falkland Islands. Used to ferrying aristocrats and royalty, Scott-Masson would now carry the third Battalion of the Parachute Regiment and 40 Commando of the Royal Marines, where we had finally been assigned.

I don't know exactly where the SS Canberra first earned its nickname, "The Great White Whale," but to take one look at the massive cruise liner, there is no wondering why it stuck. At over two hundred and fifty meters in length, with a beam of thirty-one meters, she is a mammoth sight to behold on approach through the water.

When I was informed that our transport assignment would be aboard the SS Canberra, I was over the moon. Of course we would ride in style.

Most of the lads were assigned to beds on E deck, located below the water line. These were the quarters normally reserved for the ship's grunts, the laundry and kitchen staff; military brass stayed in the rooms up above. Although they were only humble servant's accommodations, no one cared. While on board, we would be afforded at least a glimpse of how the other half lived.

The mounting international tensions that eventually led into the Falkland Island War had, for my mates at least, become a curious string of luxury accommodations. Boarding the ship, we could hardly believe our bizarre fortune. First, we had been housed as so-called prisoners of war at a cushy beachfront hotel in Uruguay. Sure we had gotten a stern bollicking from command for the day's events, but in the end, we had been fed beer and steak, like royalty. Then a mountain top villa awaited us.

Now on our way back to the front, we were regaled with a cruise ship. The sleeping quarters were larger than we were accustomed to, with clean, functional bathrooms that didn't give you the shivers to step into. For a short while at least, we were granted the dignity of taking a crap in private, with the doors closed. A few weeks before, society's elite dined and slept on the Canberra; now it was the lot of us.

There were various bars located throughout the ship's decks. Belly up to these was were where most of us could be found killing the little time we had without obligation. We were offered a beer and trivia night to occupy our time.

Gambling and card games were popular. The gaming tables felt like a Mediterranean casino floor, only without pit boss supervision. No one would back down if they felt that the other guy was cheating or running a con. Defending the Crown sounded like a lovely sentiment, but we were all there to make as much scratch as we possibly could. The SS Canberra had been assigned a military band that offered a variety of live music, marches or pop or classical.

We played games on deck during daylight hours, tug of war or the like. We took a fancy to schoolyard games, anything we could use to blow off steam, and there was a lot of that mounting below the surface. One afternoon, we held a 10K race on the deck, where participants were cheered lustily on by their respective companies and branches.

Naturally, we spent a good amount of our time in formal training. We would not be allowed to lose focus on our mission. We drilled hard on combat proficiencies, weapon handling, field skills, and aircraft recognition. Regiments of the Royal Artillery were on board SS Canberra as well, and they gave the lads in rifle section an opportunity to call down mortar fire. As the ship cut south through rough, windy seas, we prepared ourselves for the harsh climate that awaited us. Just facing into the wind gave you a taste of the awful weather that awaited us in the Falklands.

We worked on building up core strength through rigorous training. Our legs, feet and backs had to arrive on land in topnotch shape if we were going to survive the second round of combat. Some of the lads groused. Not me. I loved to train. The sheer drive to improve was never dim with me, even when surrounded by relative opulence as we were. Whenever I could find the spare time, I dropped for a quick set of push-ups, sit-ups or squats. I would do anything to gain an edge.

And when there was nothing assigned for us to do, we "yomped." The British press covering the journey took quite a shine to the term and started using it here and there in pieces covering our journey south.

Yomping is a term that we came up with for the sound we made running around in full equipment atop the deck. We were quite a sight.

I imagine those citizens back home got a good chuckle, reading about a lot of soldiers grunting and howling while running in and out of a maze of lounge chairs.

Quite absurd to those unfamiliar, I'm sure.

Nothing about my involvement in the Falkland Island War

had played normally. Perhaps that is one of the greatest misconceptions of warfare: the presumption of normalcy.

Movement of the British task force did not go unnoticed. Something as daunting as a military task force is a hard thing to keep a secret.

As we cut southward through the seas off the coast of South America, our position remained under close observation by the junta. At night, the task force ships were ordered to darken, but during daylight, we moved out in the open. Ship positions were constantly varied, sometimes kept close in tight; other times, we were miles apart. Regardless of our effort, there was no hiding the sheer size of something so large.

The Argentinean Air Force was constantly patrolling the skies around the task force. From time to time, they would order a squadron of reconnaissance jets over the top of our position, jets buzzing our heads. Amid the constant chopper noise and deep roar of the ship's engine, the sound of approaching fighters was distinct, sounding alarms and sending a pulse of anticipation throughout the ship.

Whenever an Argentinean recon sortie approached, an Air Red order was broadcast over the ship's main intercom. Air Red meant simply that a gunner was to run up from his quarters to the top deck with his GPMG ready. Once he was there, he would get off whatever shot he could manage at the plane flying overhead.

An Air Red was a burst of pure madness. I can still remember the jolt to life those words gave me. As a gunner, Air Red meant that I had to cover a long distance just to get into position. Up from my bunk on E Deck, I would grab my equipment, race down the hall, through the engine and boiler rooms toward the stern of the ship before I even reached the stairway. There it was multiple stories to get outside. So much running left me absolutely knackered, and the call of Air Red became an annoyance.

To this day, I have no bloody idea why a GPMG gunner was not stationed on the deck of the SS Canberra around the clock. I may have been able to take one of those annoying jets down from time to time if I had been stationed there, gun already trained skyward. Often on an Air Red, I wouldn't even get a decent shot off, only a quick burst of gunfire at a vanishing plane. I never hit one, and the Argentineans never bombed us. For the time being, they got exactly what they needed, intelligence.

What I did get from an Air Red though was a view of the task force. Although seldom, a few times over those days at sea, twenty ships could be glimpsed from the deck, a row of ten or more spread out from each side of the SS Canberra as we navigated through the chop. We knew what was around us, but to see it was another matter.

The troop carrying ships, SS Canberra along with Elk, Europic Ferry, and Norland were, aside from a few GPMG gunners, defenseless. Consequently, we were nestled in the middle. Forming that protective shell around us, I can still remember the names of many of those assault ships without looking them up:

Fearless, Intrepid, and Argonaut, to name just a few.

The task force was heading straight into the harsh Atlantic autumn. Whenever the seas became rough, I remember those military ships rolled like corks.

Not us though. The SS Canberra moved smoothly, no matter the conditions.

I wasn't thinking in broad, historical terms back then. Although I had, in military terms, become an old sweat, I had yet to attain an old man's perspective.

I have that now.

In hindsight, I am left to wonder whether that British task force on its way to the Falkland Islands didn't stand for something more than a show of military force.

Perhaps that mobilization was the last time such a massive fleet of ships and men will move in such a way.

We simply do not fight wars like this anymore.

There was a theater on board SS Canberra with movies running twenty-four hours a day. Cinema had a soothing affect and someone high above me in the ranks knew quite well what to show in order to keep Marines entertained over many long days at sea. Mostly, we were offered a limited assortment of the latest skin and war movies. Notorious American porno flick, "Deep Throat" went up on the big screen quite a bit and was always well received by the lads. There was no trapping to be done on board and our prospects for finding female company in the near future looked dim. We had to exercise our fantasies somewhere. I'm sure a few of the church going guys avoided it, but most of us got a titillating chuckle out of Linda Lovelace's dubious performance as a woman who possessed, politely stated, uncommon oral sex skills. I still laugh out loud when I think of the line, "the end, and deep throat to you all."

Adult entertainment wasn't the extent of what the cinema showed. I also sat through several showings of "Cross of Iron" during that long journey, a much different movie starring a cast of luminary actors—James Mason, James Coburn, and Maximillian Schell. It is a film that I could not get enough of and can still today quote verbatim, even though I have not seen it in years. Directed by Sam Peckinpah, a great many moments out of that 1977 World War two classic have become synonymous with my time on board SS Canberra. One scene that I think of as particularly iconic for my frame of mind at the time is the movie's final confrontation, wherein a Russian boy soldier shoots Schell as he struggles awkwardly to reload his weapon. There is a deep sense of reality in "Cross of Iron." We'd all heard the tales from WWII vets and the movie felt sympathetic to one of those stories. Producers used authentic tanks and equipment. There is also a coldblooded ironic twist in the end that I could certainly appreciate.

The showings of war movies were, for obvious reasons, more calmly received. The images of men shot down lent a somber tone, even though we were all aware they were actors following a script. We all knew what we were heading into; war is war, even if it's not one of the so-called great European conflicts from a generation ago.

Lads took the message to heart. They really listened to what was said and done. There was no hooting and hollering as Coburn's cruel, harrowing laughter bellowed on and images of dead civilians rolled under the credits.

The line from the end about seeing "where the crosses of iron grow" still gives me goose bumps.

Officers took meals in the SS Canberra's first class restaurant, still adorned with its glittery lights and chandeliers. This left a second dining hall for everyone else.

Many of the most memorable scenes from aboard SS Canberra took place in that dining hall. Cushy seats, real dinner plates that you might be proud to serve your mother on, clean silverware. Mealtimes had all the trappings of a decent vacation.

While we didn't exactly feast during that journey, the meals we were served turned out to be more appetizing than the loads of utter shite we had been shoveled back on base, and we knew they would be far better than the rations we would be forced to survive on after landing in the Falkland Islands. We were allowed to feast before being reduced to mere subsistence. The lads often talked about how grateful they were for a bite of grub that had the look and taste of real food. There was a regular wine service for the grunts as well, enough of a pour for a proper drink with your meal.

What made the scenes from that dining hall so memorable was its role as center stage for a simmering rivalry that had sprang up on SS Canberra. The lines in the bitter feud between the paratroopers and Marines had been drawn, almost instantly. Every soldier on board seemed to live in a constant face off, across the line from one another and it began the moment we walked up the plank to get on board.

The competition between rival military factions ends up looking a lot like a pair of brothers close in age. Perhaps it's best to think in terms of football squads facing one another on the pitch, except everyone plays for the same team. We are all British, ostensibly driven by the same sense of purpose. We wanted to survive and win the war, and in this case, return the Falkland Islands to their rightful hands. One might think that common objective would be a cause for harmony, but that is simply not the case.

For the Royal Marines and Parachute regiments, parts of the Navy and Army respectively, there is quite a bit of overlap in the type of man that rises in each branch. Every one of us had it drilled into our heads that we were counted as the best of the best, her Majesty's cream; no one was going to cede that mantle without putting up one hell of a fight. We were whole units where even the very last in line was a tough guy. Perhaps we ended up so damn hard on one another because we were, in truth, too similar to link arms.

Straight out of basic training, the toughest guy out of each branch rises and assumes the role as an Alpha. It's a hard earned distinction, one that is thrust into immediate peril when two units are blended together on a ship for days on end. Suddenly, the pecking order needs sorting out.

And what do Alpha males do better besides prove themselves? When we weren't ogling Linda Lovelace, or champing at the bit for the battlefield after watching "Iron Crosses," there were tousles, punches slipped and what felt like constant shouting matches. Everyone was on edge. Without the Argentine army to face off against at the end of a rifle, we were all desperate to prove ourselves the superior group.

A few times, things with the Paras turned downright nasty.

Ottawan is a French pop duo that hardly anyone talks about anymore, but mere mention of the band's name sticks in my craw. In 1980, Ottawan managed to climb up the European charts with a smash hit, "Hands Up (Give Me Your Heart)," a song that has long been lost to the obscurity of time. Disco was never really my cup of tea but at the time, the song was pretty catchy and all of the girls liked it. We would hear it while out at the clubs on leave or the weekends. The song took on a different meaning aboard the SS

Canberra though. A few times during training, the lads in the Parachute Regiments broke with yomping and regaled the Marines of NP8901 with a full-throated serenade of that bloody song. Hands up. Surrender. The bastards. I can still hear them now.

For me, that song has not been lost to time. It remains inexorably woven into many of my strongest memories of the war. Music is like that.

There they all were, up on deck, our own brothers in arms, prancing around like ponies and outwardly ridiculing 45 Commando for surrendering control of the Falklands. They were rubbing our noses in shite for the indignity of walking out with our hands up, for forcing everyone back to fight again. What I wouldn't have done for a quick blast of some punk rock, something by the UK Subs to throw back at them.

And what was the worst part of that mocking ritual? We had no choice but to stand there and take it on the chin. Sons of bitches. It was a tough pill to swallow.

I did my best to stay cool, but from time to time, my temper got the best of me. It's hard to keep a level head, cooped up like we were.

The Paras were merciless in teasing us. While drinking at one of the bars, they would call us out, mocking us as cross-dressing surrender monkeys. It only took a couple of days at sea before that joke became rotten. Turn the other cheek? That kind of advice only really works if you have somewhere to go.

I took a jab or two, but I wasn't taking any of it lying down. They were green but that hardly mattered. Without convenient counter, my best response was usually a nasty comment of some kind, usually about how bad the guy was stinking up the place.

"You fucking stink, mate. Like shite. Try and take a bath once in a while."

Rivalry was not the full extent of our interactions. Although we had indeed been routed off the island under dubious circumstance, we remained the only detachment that had seen action. We knew what the fight was going to be like on the Falklands.

We took great pride in that distinction. Often the Paras would come to us with their questions. They wanted to know what they were in for.

Whenever one of the Paras asked me about the firefight, I told them what I knew. Wasn't much to speak of, but pride wouldn't get in the way of sharing my view.

Sure, the Paras gave us a strong ration of shit that felt like a punch in the gut, but no one was going to be a son of a bitch about it.

Our journey was highly publicized back at home. We became something of a sideshow for the conflict at large, a human-interest story to sell papers.

News spread even further. Stories of the SS Canberra went out to news bureaus all across the globe; not just English speaking countries either. Everyone seemed to be taking an interest in the story of how 40 and 45 Commando of the Marines, and the Third Parachute Regiment, ended up on board a luxury liner.

There was a keen interest in spreading news of our approach to leaders in the Argentine military junta. British ministers of information were careful that any information pertaining to the growing task force reached Buenos Aires.

The show of might was ready to wage war, but only if its muscle couldn't prevent its start.

However ready we were to avenge our shame, I believe deep down that every single lad held out some hope the junta would eventually do the wise thing, however faint. Maybe I am wrong, but there was not a morning where I did not wake up, pining to hear the news that the Argentines had simply packed up and backed out of the Falkland Islands altogether.

One thing was certain: if we went ashore, lives would be lost. We wouldn't get out unscathed again. Quite likely, more than a few lads would die there. Bloodless victory is a victory nonetheless, and we hoped the sheer speed of mobilization and the might we brought forth into the South Atlantic would be enough of a convincer.

As the April days dragged on toward the Ides though, there was little indication my wish for a bloodless end would come true. If the Argentine junta was indeed fearful, they were doing a breakout job of keeping it close to the vest.

I think it's funny how your memory flashes back. It either arrives back in a flutter or a roar; it never seems to come in the middle.

Something once thought lost is suddenly found again and it becomes quite difficult to comprehend how it ever went away.

Our lives are absolutely pot holed with these curious glimpses.

As I get a little older and I find an increasing need to reconcile some of what I have done with my life, these glimpses come to me more frequently.

Fifteen odd years after the end of the war, my thoughts

of the events of the spring of 1982 were fleeting at best. I had long since moved on. Life demanded that my attention direct itself elsewhere, but I remember reading a snippet story in the news:

The SS Canberra had at last reached the end of its seafaring life. Its final voyage had ended unceremoniously on Halloween night, 1997. The old ocean liner, by now nearly forty years in age, ancient in luxury terms, was scheduled for decommissioning, after which it would be sent to Pakistan, where it would be scrapped.

I laughed. Torn to bits for a lifetime of service. Sounds like what life eventually has in store for us all.

I did a little investigating on the name the news article gave. As it turns out, a lot of vessels like that find their end in the Gadani ship-breaking yard.

The brief but critical role that the SS Canberra played as a troop carrier was mentioned, however briefly, in the ship's obituary. Perhaps that voyage was the only real reason that the death of a luxury liner, surely replaced by some bigger, faster and newer ship, would ever find its way into the news for public consideration.

I'm not given to nostalgia, like some men my age. Sentimental is not really the best way to describe the feeling when I read the news.

It was more of a twinge. When I imagined The Great White Whale leaving port for one last time, I was reminded of how bittersweet life can be.

And there is a cruelty to it as well.

Somewhere amid the rusted hulks of a thousand other vessels deemed obsolete, some working stiff was going to pull her hull apart, on hands and knees, with a crowbar pulling whatever parts off of her might be valuable.

He would likely never know the sound of yomping, nor would he feel the fevered pitch of a rivalry between regiments.

Linda Lovelace. James Coburn.

Their images have long since moved off the screen, to the fleeting memories of the lads who, for a brief time, called her home.

Chapter 9
Shock and Awe

War is fought as much over the airwaves as it is by men in the trenches. Maintaining strict control over information isn't simply propaganda. It is as vital to victory as protecting ammunition or supply lines.

This has always been true, at least to some extent. Even back in medieval times, that firm grasp on the message is what divides the heroic kings from the tyrants.

Every day through the end of April, the BBC would give regular updates on the evolving situation in the Falklands. As one of the most widely broadcast and translated programs on the entire planet, the title "world service" isn't just a clever tag line.

Aside from the generals and majors, none of the lads on board the SS Canberra were privy to any special information. We were kept reasonably well-informed though. At the very least, we were fed a similar story to the world at large.

A 24-hour TV news cycle had yet to evolve into reality. Back in 1982, television still went off the air each night. Consequently, there was no CNN to turn to.

Soldiers deployed away from England grow accustomed to huddling together over the radio each day. Those stories and features, however small, are our lifeblood, the only real connection to the goings on at home. On the SS Canberra, the radio gave us access to information about political discussions, those that were supposedly taking place behind closed doors. We heard items about the heads in the UK and Argentine governments working hard to hammer out a peaceful end to the brewing conflict.

The sensitive negotiations lumbered on. We heard a few reports that American officials had taken their seat at the table, news that was met with conflicted feelings. One thing remains true: on the geo-political scene, our Uncle Sam always finds his way to the table. He sits there, boldly waving his red, white, and blue banner in hopes of assuring that his economic and strategic interests are well taken care of.

Some of us bristled at the news. Since World War II, Uncle Sam had become like a big brother. We were proud. An American protector was a reality none of us wanted.

Perhaps though, that intervention would result in a peaceful end.

As days at sea dragged into what felt at times like oblivion, I felt my personal interest in those negotiations slowly increase. Whenever the radio came on, I listened more closely to what was being said. On the off chance that I missed any crucial details, I went back to listen again. I asked around. The idea of fighting a war with the junta did not frighten me, nor did the idea of being away from home. I was, however, optimistic that things would turn in the direction of a diplomatic finish.

My sense of optimism was regularly tested. Although those BBC World Report broadcasts were filled with stories and what were trumped up as fresh perspectives on that diplomatic solution, it sounded, at least to me, like those negotiations had reached a standstill. No one had gotten up from the table. But weeks later, nothing had evolved.

As the SS Canberra crept closer to the Falkland Islands, I had to face up with reality. The BBC World Report was indeed news, but it was state sanitized news. We heard what we were supposed to hear. Our crown and government, although we were sworn to protect them, were like any other global power poised on the brink of war. They were interested in the prestige of public opinion; no one wanted to be seen as the bully. What we heard when we huddled around the radio were public relations crafted stories—only that information which had been deemed fit for our consumption, as well as the world at large. What was actually going on? The truth was anyone's guess.

In spite of our on-going role as mushrooms, there remained a faint glimmer of hope in the lads on the SS Canberra. Some were itching for a fight, but they were a minority. Perhaps that optimism wasn't drawn from what we heard or were told. Perhaps that ray of hope came from elsewhere, an optimistic belief that when given the opportunity to choose, men will take the easier, more peaceful route over war.

No one uttered those sorts of sentiments out loud. We were all bloody soldiers. Most of us had been in a firefight. We knew what came next, and no one wanted to be pegged as soft. No one wanted to give the guy next to him any reason to doubt.

Still, you could see the disappointment. It was written on the faces. It was conveyed in the forlorn sighs that came every time the news turned up empty.

Whatever hopes we might have had, we clung to desperately as the calendar switched over into May. Then all that hope blew over in a rather sudden manner.

Although the task force was very close to the Falklands, we were still aboard the SS Canberra on the morning of the second of May.

What we heard over the radio proved to be the clarion call that we had all, in one way or another, been dreading.

"The United Kingdom stayed on the attack in the South Atlantic this morning," the taciturn reporter said. "And Argentina may have suffered a grievous loss of life."

Everyone stopped cold and lingered on the next line.

"Late this afternoon, the government reported that the cruiser, the General Belgrano, is presumed to have sunk."

This news struck us hard, like a lead weight. Her sinking was the last prelude to an all-out war over the Falklands; this one, however, was not so subtle.

Named after Manuel Belgrano, one of Argentina's founding fathers, the ARA General Belgrano was their navy's only cruiser and the second largest ship in their fleet. Purchased from the United States in 1951, the junta had repurposed a vessel that had been decommissioned and sent to Philadelphia, destined for the scrap yard. In her second life in service to the South American nation, the ARA General Belgrano grew to significant acclaim, officially earning her ultimate name in the days after her contribution to the 1955 overthrow of President Juan Peron.

Among the first actions taken by the British on April second was the designation of a Maritime Exclusion Zone, two hundred miles in every direction around the Falkland Islands. Outside that zone, Argentinean wartime vessels were deemed safe; inside, they risked attack from the nuclear-powered submarines patrolling those waters. On April 23rd, that message was even further clarified in the Swiss Embassy in Buenos Aires. A ship that entered that halo would be deemed hostile, and ultimately subject to military response. Only a week later, that Maritime Exclusion Zone was redefined as a "Total Exclusion Zone," meaning that any penetration by aircraft would be considered hostile as well.

While the British task force crept south toward Ascension Island, the Argentinean junta reinforced the units already dug into position on the Falklands. As a result, two Argentinean task forces were deployed east to the islands, 79.1 with an aircraft carrier and another, 79.2 armed with heavy missile capability.

From Ushala on April 26th, a port in Tierra Del Fuego on the southern tip of Argentina, considered the southernmost city in the world, the ARA General Belgrano launched on a northern course, where it met up to form a third task force.

During those last few days of April 1982, the presence of the new task force, 79.3, led by the ARA General Belgrano, had become troublesome. They didn't simply skirt the southern curve of the total exclusion zone. They made incursions.

In hindsight, these bold overtures of war could not be any clearer.

Early in the Falkland conflict, a considerable portion of British strategy had been devoted to provocation, sometimes not so gently. We wanted the Argentines to make the first move. It was the clear strategic view of the British that it would prove far more advantageous in a global sense if the junta were seen as again initiating the conflict.

Good PR always finds a way into the equation.

Adversaries in relatively close quarters create problems. As the calendar turned into May, a few skirmishes began. British piloted Vulcan bombers patrolled areas inside of the exclusion zone, ever closer to the disputed islands. Long-range bombs were lobbed through the sea air from distances of more than a thousand meters out, targeted for the Argentine held airport on the eastern end of Stanley. All together, several hundred tons of ordnance landed on the airfield, a considerable amount that was not quite enough to fully disable it. Slowly, the plan of provocation started to bear its fruit. Air patrols launched from 79.3 eventually took the bait. They started engaging with British patrols, fighting that went on and off through the May Day afternoon.

Late that afternoon, the ARA General Belgrano carrier task force moved in south of the Falkland Islands, inside the exclusion zone. It was well known by that time where the strength in the Argentine Navy was held. The ARA General Belgrano was equipped with Exocet missiles, firepower that presented a clear and present threat to ships in the British task force around Ascension Island. From a considerable range, the ARA General Belgrano could wreak havoc on the vulnerable ships.

Royal Navy Rear Admiral Sandy Woodward, commander of the Hermes aircraft carrier group, simply would not allow that threat to manifest.

In war, soldiers like me only know what's in front of them. A lot happens out of sight, a lot that affects what comes next.

By the early morning hours on May 2nd, Argentinean task

force 79.3 had already been engaged in a risky game of cat and mouse that had gone on for a couple of days. Whether or not the task force knew it, they were being stalked by the Conqueror, a British nuclear powered submarine, what one might refer to as a giant killer.

On May first, Admiral Juan Lombardo ordered all Argentine naval units to hone in on the British task force. He made clear overtures that they would launch a massive attack on the following day. Unbeknownst to Lombardo, that crucial message was intercepted by British intelligence, and it spurred Thatcher and her War Cabinet to make pleas with the chief of the defense staff to abruptly alter the rules of engagement; she wanted the green light to attack the ARA General Belgrano outside the exclusion zone.

The threat was clear. An attack was imminent. Exclusion zone or not, a counter attack was necessary.

Captain Chris Wreford-Brown, captain of the Conqueror submarine, agreed. Thatcher got her go-ahead.

On May second, the ARA General Belgrano cut a jagged course near Rio Grande Air Base, positioned along the southern edge of the exclusion zone, an area known as Burdwood Bank. Due directly east of Isla de los Estados, consisting of roughly one thousand square miles of shallow waters, Burdwood Bank was not believed to be deep enough to allow the successful navigation of a nuclear submarine.

Lombardo and his advisors believed that this area was an ideal place to keep the ARA General Belgrano hidden. The cruiser could lurk quietly until darkness fell, when they could cut up north, a quick trip into Exocet missile range of the task force.

The main player in the Argentinean attack was in position.

Eight Argentine A-4 Skyhawk jets were activated on the morning of May second. They were armed with bombs and fueled up for a medium range mission. Fatefully that morning, there was a light wind in the South Atlantic, enough to prevent the heavy planes from launching. Then, slowly, the Argentinean carrier group moved discretely along the Burwood Bank, until they were well out of range of British reconnaissance.

In the moments before 1900 on May second, Admiral John Forster "Sandy" Woodward stepped outside of the regimented chain of command. Although Captain Wreford-Brown had already given his okay to jump the rules of engagement, the torpedo launch was not Woodward's call to make. Woodward's choice to act was in defiance, unmistakably, but it was one that he would be recognized as a hero for. Later in his career, he was knighted Sir John Forster Woodward, and has gone into naval lore as an inspirational figure.

Woodward gave an order to the Conqueror. That order was then relayed up to the War Cabinet. "Fire on the General Belgrano", he had said.

The order was quickly confirmed.

At a range of 1,400 yards, just over one and a quarter kilometers, the Conqueror fired a spread of three Mark 8 torpedoes; two of those struck the stern of the unsuspecting destroyer. The General Belgrano, an old ship that had been first commissioned as the USS Phoenix and survived the Japanese attack on Pearl Harbor, exploded into an ascendant ball of flame. It was a torrent of fire that lit up the dim sky.

The ship began to sink toward the bow. Captain Bonzo

immediately ordered the crew to abandon ship. Witnesses to the disaster said that evacuation proceeded in a calm and orderly manner in spite of the inferno. Multiple distress signals were launched, but the sky was too dim for the two escort vessels to see them. The ARA General Belgrano sank in the icy waters south of Burdwood Bank in under an hour.

By the next morning, the numbers were broadcast to the world. Over three hundred Argentine lives had been lost.

Decades after the sinking of ARA General Belgrano, through a revisionist's lens, critics belied the attack as unwarranted. In spite of the message of clear menace intercepted from Lombardo the day prior, an Argentinean attack was not imminent.

Even if 79.3 was preparing for an eventual move against the Task Force, critics of Thatcher and the military called the old ship incapable. They derided ARA General Belgrano as a museum piece that had long ago passed its relevance. Nothing rescued from the bone yards of Philadelphia could present a real danger to the Royal Navy.

Woodward did not see the ARA General Belgrano as a helpless relic, nor was his interpretation of Lombardo's message as toothless talk.

To Rear Admiral Woodward, a menace should be taken seriously. Woodward gave the order to fire, and hours later, any debate was already over.

Whatever damage either figure may have been able to exact on the British task force is a mystery whose answer is lost to time. Luckily, it never became an issue.

The sinking of the ARA General Belgrano proved an important moment for two distinct reasons. The surprise attack turned the notch of conflict, from skirmish up to a full-fledged war, but it also served as a critical blow to the junta.

In the days following, the Argentinean navy would retreat west, back to their bases. They would not play a role in the coming conflict.

Consequently, carrier borne military aircraft were forced to launch from assorted land bases in Argentina, only able to operate within the limits of their range. This allowed British submarines and ships free rein to patrol the waters around the islands. The junta lost considerable credibility and power back home in Buenos Aires.

And this also opened the door for the British invasion of the Falklands. We would be back on land in a matter of hours.

There is an unmistakable banality to war. Only in hindsight, though, can a soldier actually see that for what it is. There is no panic, no immediate sense of dread. News that the General Belgrano had been sunk spread like wildfire throughout the task force but life, to some extent, went on as it always does.

What felt different now, however, was that the lads were aware. Our optimism had been dispatched with that sinking ship.

We all knew we were bound for the role of invading force.

That night, I drank and played cards. A bunch of lads had decided to gather down in the mess room. There were a lot of familiar faces in the lot. I remember Gaz and Eggman there, laughing and reading each other the riot act. These were the same lads that I had surrendered with at Government House just over a month ago.

The other lads were rowdy as well. There were no longer illusions of harmony. Perhaps that starkness is what punched up the spirit of everyone there. We were aware that we were going back to that sodden island, and all its blistering wind, to fight the Argentines, and there was no turning back. Every one of us was piss full, but there was a sense of normalcy to it as well. Sinking or none, we'd likely have done the same.

I took my mates for a few hundred pounds that night back and stumbled up to my bunk. We had been playing a game called three-card brag, an old version of poker that was based on bluffing the other players. I was never much of a card shark. Walking away from the table with a fat pocket felt pretty damn good.

The next day, we were all up early. Our commander gave us a very specific set of instructions. In no uncertain terms, we were ordered to each write a good-bye letter. Something, he said, that would be addressed to the soldier's next of kin.

Take a few moments. Go ahead. Give your family a personal message, a few sentiments that they can take some pride in, in case that you are killed in action.

No one had expressed a fear of battle. This sobering request, however, stole what was left of that rowdy mood out from under us, to say the very least.

During my time in the service, I never took much of a shine on letter writing. Even in the good times, I figured it was better to take it all in and tell the story later.

Now, suddenly, as the rest of my mates retired to scribble down their heartfelt good-bye to mother and father, wife and girlfriend, I found that I was all twisted up.

I was never much of an effusive guy. Frankly, I didn't quite know what emotions I felt in that moment. Even if I could identify them, I wasn't quite sure that I could write them down on command.

What the bloody hell am I going to say? I remember thinking, twirling the pen around in my fingers. Wasn't I still alive and well, after all?

How the hell was I supposed to know what I would want anyone to know? Especially my parents?

Dear Mom and Dad, I fought bravely. I love you guys. God save the fucking queen, if you're reading this, I'm already dead.

Every way that I started the letter in my head felt hollow.

As torn up as I was over what I would say, I was never one to buck command. Maybe I had been something of a smart ass as a young man, but I was an old sweat by this point, and I knew quite well that this wasn't the kind of thing to raise hell about.

Reluctantly, I sat down with my pen and a sheet of paper. I took that stack of card winnings from my safe box and set every last one of those three hundred pound notes into an envelope and then sealed it up, accompanied by a handwritten note.

Dad,

If you get this, then you know what happened. Have a drink on me.

Your son.

I can still see the letters on the page now. However brief, however lacking in sentiment, those were my feelings in that moment before going off to war.

PART III: Tumble Down

Chapter 10
Making Landfall

I handed the letter over to Major Mike Norman. Like the rest of the lads in my section, I was suddenly confronted with the uncertainty of what my fate would be. What would come of those three hundred pounds? Would Dad ever open that letter or would it, like a boomerang, come back to me?

Our section was informed that we would soon be making our long anticipated landfall on the Falkland Islands. Although we were kept in the dark and not told exactly when our time would come, I could tell by the sudden spike in activity that we would be moving some time in the next few hours.

Finally, there was some excitement. We would get to see a little action.

All of the lads in NP8901 began preparations by packing up their gear. We had been given what was referred to as a fighting order; equipment like ammunition for our weapons, detailed maps of the terrain, a compass and a radio, and a backup set of batteries. For the most part, everyone carried the same fighting order, with some slight variation relative to weapon and their battlefield function.

Even though I had seen battle, I was still pretty green when compared to the rest of the section. In my short time in service, I had not yet earned enough money to upgrade my gear. Some of the older guys packed up their good sleeping bags, a decent down jacket, or something made from Gore-Tex that would shed the rain.

Unfortunately, at the time of the Falkland Island war, all of my stuff was still standard issue, which meant barely good enough.

We were given personal discretion on how to pack for landfall beyond our fighting order. How many extra shirts or pairs of socks that a Marine brought was up to them, as were other choices, say between bringing deodorant, a shaving kit or a toothbrush. If you could manage to fit it all into your Bergen rucksack (what we used to call Alpine-style backpacks back then), and carry it on your back, according to command, go ahead.

A few guys made what seemed to me like peculiar choices. I remember Jim McKay packing up a frying pan that he had bought. I had a good laugh when I saw that, wondering whether he thought he was going to cook up a fancy sort of meal in the bloody Falkland grass. Maybe he thought that if he got into it with an Argentinean commando, he could knock him back, using the cast iron as a blunt force weapon.

The only thing we were forbidden to pack into our Bergens was a personal keepsake: expressly stated, no pictures or letters from loved ones.

Maybe at first blush such a mandate seemed a little harsh, but our command had our best interests in mind. They were trying to protect anyone who might get captured from harsh, psychological interrogations. I suppose the logic was, the less those bastards know about your family, the better. For some of the lads in my section, leaving those things behind was a bitter reality. After all, those were the people they were fighting to return home to. On my end though, I didn't care. I had not carried those types of sentimental objects with me into the South Atlantic anyway. The way I saw it, more room for socks, three pairs of wool, a tin cup to cook in, and a water bottle.

Making sure you have sufficient food is a big part of packing for landfall. Royal Marines were issued our sustenance in the form of 24-hour ration packs. The military packs five thousand calories into a plain cardboard box, along with tea. Ration packs contained a mushy mixture of dehydrated meat, usually a few unappetizing chunks of mutton, potatoes, and curry, and a vegetable, all of it broken out into four labeled compartments, A through D. A soldier could eat it cold, or depending on the situation, warm their meal up in a cup or by lighting the little heating blocks that were packed in.

Field rations are pretty bland stuff; some of the lads groused about them, but they did not bother me too much. I had always seen food as fuel for my body. Eating was something that I did to survive, not necessarily an endeavor I was keen on waiting around and savoring. That holds true even today. Sure, I'll eat a good meal if it's offered to me, but fine dining just is not a priority.

The way I saw it, carrying two or three packs of slop meant that I had enough food to keep me alive for the few days it would take for us to get more.

Everyone knew what was coming for us. When we finally made our landfall on San Carlos, we would be in for a fight. In those last few hours at sea packing up, talk within the section was loose and free. Gaz and I cracked a few jokes whenever we saw the opportunity, our dark sense of humor keeping us from getting too worked up.

I don't remember that there was a lot of sentiment going around the boat. What I do recall, though, was a bunch of lads asking, how long is this going to last?

When are we going to get home?

Is it going to be September?

On the idea of getting home early, I was pessimistic. The real possibility that we could get stuck down here as late as November had crept into the back of my mind.

Once again though, I wasn't terribly bent out of shape about any of it.

I was just nineteen years old. The wait ended and a movement order was given, so I pulled my Bergen on and followed the man in front of me to the troop transport.

I was living for the moment. This was an adventure.

In war, waiting can often be the worst part. It's in the quiet moments in between when your worst thoughts can get the best of you.

Our troop transport, an old World War II styled aquatic vehicle, touched down in the icy waters off of Falkland Sound. We were near San Carlos.

The time was a little bit past 1000 hours. Although I was relieved to finally be off the Canberra and in motion, an eerie thought came over me.

I could hear Argentinean jets screaming; from which direction they came was difficult to determine though. Out of instinct, a few of the lads ducked and covered their heads. I could see bursts of light from the explosions; we felt the vibrations as bombs exploded on British ship positions all up and down "bomb alley." For that whole boat ride, our field of view was exclusively over our heads. I could not see the explosion from the bomb's impact, only the sudden change in color as the sky filled with flames.

We were out in the open, prone to enemy attack. At this moment, I thought we are completely vulnerable, just like in a floating coffin.

No one could see the water lapping against the outside of the craft, nor did we have a point of view on the action on the shore we were fast approaching. Whether or not we were in for a hot landing when we finally got to Green Beach, not even Lou, our leader, could say with any certainty. We had no bloody idea if we would be mowed down by Argentinean gunfire as soon as the gates lowered, or if we would find the beach quiet.

No one spoke a word. Our nerves girded to the uncertain sounds of warfare. Even black humor cannot suffice in moments like this. We must have been on that transport for at least fifteen minutes, enough time to huff down a couple of smokes.

As we got closer to shore, word came down that we would have a dry landing. That meant the vehicle gate would drop on sand instead of in the sound.

When it finally did open, though, we were instantly up to our necks in seawater. Someone had fucked up the calculation. Within a matter of seconds, our bodies and everything that we carried were soaked, and there was no way to escape the icy water.

There was no time to grouse about our condition though. We charged toward shore blindly, through the water, up onto our beachhead, where we crossed the sand and dove into a defensive position against stands of tussock grass as tall as a man.

I closed my eyes and took a deep breath. I slowed down my racing heart and did my best to gather my bearings. There had been no gunfire greeting. Perhaps we had managed to make landfall without detection by the Argentineans.

I watched as the transport vehicle backed away from shore. As it turned back around in the surf to pick up its next group of soldiers, I realized we were all alone.

The fight for survival began right now.

While the intense fighting continued on Bomb Alley, the beach remained relatively quiet. With the threat of a hot landing gone, we were able to make a few preliminary preparations. We still had a panoramic view of the Sound. I could see the Argentinean jets flying overhead, bombing our boats. There was no time to sit back and watch though.

Our orders were to dig what were called shell scrapes into the sand against the tussock grass. A shell scrape is a dug out, wide enough for two soldiers to lay down side by side and plenty deep, so that their positions would be hidden from anyone approaching on the beach. We pulled the spades out of our fighting order and got busy.

For a few hours, Gaz and I worked diligently at the chore of digging; cursing at the chore was a little more like it though. Getting a spade into that rocky, dense, peat packed ground was nothing short of brutal. I would have thought we could move faster digging into the center lane of a London street, but we managed. Gaz and I took turns. One of us dug frantically while the other rested and kept a watch over.

Once everyone in our section had finished digging out their

shell scrape and were safely hidden inside, that old spirit of friendship came roaring back. Voices shouted back and forth between dugouts, ten or fifteen meters apart along the bank.

"Can you believe that?"

"Did you see over there?"

Our orders were to remain dark, which meant that we could not light anything to heat our tea, but we could steep it cold.

"Anyone have any sugar?"

We managed to share comic moments to keep morale up. Looking around at our sullen accommodations, Gaz and I had a thorough laugh. We bagged out and got some sleep when we could. We gave one another a thorough, good-natured bollicking and when an Argentinean plane flew over, we held our breath collectively till it was gone.

As I've described, sometimes the toughest part of military life is the waiting. Ninety-nine percent boredom, I thought, all for one percent action.

After a few hours settled down on Green Beach, my section finally received what would be the first of our move orders. Information came down the line from HQ that a British chopper, a Gazelle, had been taken down by an Argentine machine gunner. The aircraft had taken a hit in the engine and the rotor; HQ believed that the aircraft had managed to crash-land in a lake located in a nearby valley just beyond the ridge.

Just that little bit was enough of a spark to get us fired up. All of our boredom was chased away the instant we heard that our pilot might have been shot while trying to escape to safety in the water.

Gaz and I shared a "here we go" look as we hastily readied for the combat we had been so eager for.

Leave your packs. Take your fighting order. Get on top of that ridge.

Down at the bottom on the other side, they said we would find our downed chopper and, hopefully, a few survivors of the crash.

I packed up my gun and ammunition. I said goodbye to my Bergen. I had absolutely no idea how long it would be before I would see it again.

I had climbed a few mountains in my time. Back in those days, my back and legs were strong. I was in very tiptop condition.

Getting to the top of that ridge though? Glancing skyward, that appeared as though it would be an ordeal. The ridge we had been ordered to climb was at least a thousand feet straight up. With an elevation top to bottom of approximately one-fifth of a mile, the distance we would travel ended up being considerably further, once the sharp switchbacks and obstacle navigation were taken into consideration. A reality we would all soon learn was that any distance traveled by foot on the Falkland Islands was compounded by rugged terrain. There was no such thing as a flat, straight trek. We would be faced with stones, deep bogs and stubborn clumps of tussock grass, thick as shrubs.

The orders of engagement Lou ga ve were clear. I can still remember his words.

"Advance to contact" was his order, which meant we were all supposed to move toward the hill crest, our objective, until we took on enemy fire. If this were to happen, we would be clear to respond in kind.

Three sections began the arduous journey. There were roughly twenty men out on the mission in total. Filled with a healthy spark of anger, three sections began the yomp up the ridge side along the bay. We knew the lake's location from our maps. From our ridge-top perch, we had a wide, panoramic view of the entire valley below. If a chopper had been shot down anywhere for kilometers around us, we would be able to see the wreckage, but all around us there was nothing but rolling grassland, barren and treeless. And as we scanned the horizon, there was no chopper anywhere to be seen.

Now what the hell are we supposed to do?, I thought.

The ridge top was freezing, considerably colder than it was down on the beach. For a cup of tea, we had to scoop up a cup full of snow to boil for water.

There was a constant wind blowing in from the west; most of the time, it clocked in between ten to fifteen knots, straight into our sorry faces; it was not uncommon, though, for that wind to increase to more than forty miles per hour. At an elevation of a thousand feet, the temperature plummeted, down to around minus five degrees Celsius at night; combined with the wind, the environment was hostile, made worse by the fact that none of us was carrying a sleeping bag in our kit. Still soaking wet from our landing at San Carlos, I had never in my life been so bloody cold as I was up there.

Autumn conditions on the Falkland Islands were absolutely brutal. And as some of us wondered out loud, if we were forced to stay, how much worse would they get?

We hadn't even gotten to winter yet.

Take it, some of us said. Who the hell wants to live here anyway?

With no downed helicopter or crash survivors for us to secure, and no enemy contact to engage, we were without further order. That desolate ridge top became our position, and the three sections assumed a normal routine.

Two men at a time took a turn on watch. We ran constant patrols around the immediate vicinity of our position. We kept busy cleaning weapons and sorting gear.

Most of the rest of the time, though, we tried to find whatever way we could to dry out and get our bodies warm; this, however, proved to be a fool's errand. Our clothing was more likely to freeze solid than dry out.

Whenever we were free of watch or patrol duty, the lads found places to lie down. We wedged in side by side for warmth, in tomb like crevices between stones. We would do anything to get out of the God forsaken wind.

We had the food we landed with, but because any flame would risk giving our position away to Argentinean fighter jet patrols, we were forbidden to cook anything. Even if we were burrowed deep down in our sleeping tombs, a cook fire was considered too much of a risk, forcing us to chow down on cold rations. I gobbled down the chocolate and nuts from my ration packs and subsisted on water and cold tea.

It was a miserable day, but we had no one to lodge a complaint with. My feet were blocks of ice, but everyone in the three sections was equally cold and uncertain, so I sucked it up quietly.

I did whatever I was asked and waited with Gaz for our next order. We cracked jokes whenever we could. We ribbed each other hard. Our shared grim sense of humor kept the morale up. Our day on that ridge top was spent in wonder though.

We had been ordered to hold this position, but there was no one else around. What in the bloody hell were we doing up here anyway?

The following day, we received our answer; of course, it came in the form of new orders from HQ. All three sections were to head down to the beach, back to San Carlos, the place we started out.

Two steps forward, two steps back; I didn't much care though. At that moment, I was just grateful to get out of the wind and off of that bloody hilltop.

Maybe back down on the beach, in our shell scrape, I could finally get warm.

On May 22nd, the bulk of the British task force began consolidating its position. Our beachhead planted in the area around Green Beach and San Carlos.

With our backs pinned up against Falkland Sound and our faces firmly in the tussock grass, our section hunkered back down. We would spend a few long days without a movement order. Meanwhile, all around us, the war machine was mobilizing.

British troops, in rather large numbers, were arriving on shore. Chinook helicopters ferried heavy equipment in from our ships. Logistics were being set up at strategic points all up and down the shoreline.

The British military was establishing an overwhelming presence and as a result, our anticipation was high, but at the same time, more waiting around tempered that excitement. Although we believed that our inland press toward Stanley would begin any day, our role had been reduced to that of simple spectators.

Our section had no indication when our next move might come. Hurry up and wait. Stay in the dark. As Gaz and I joked, this was the life of a bloody mushroom.

Our ships in Bomb Alley remained under constant attack from the air. Every so often, an explosion drew our attention out toward the water.

After a few days in our shell scrapes though, even an enemy bombing came across like so much noise in the background. It became increasingly difficult to get riled up, however spectacular the sights and sounds of warfare might be.

The Argentinean flew Mirage fighters; although it seemed as though their planes were constantly streaking over our heads, they were pushed to the limits of their flight range just to get to the task force. At most, those Mirage fighters would have about five minutes to engage before having to turn around and head back to their base for fuel.

More effective than their Mirage planes were the Skyhawks. Argentinean pilots flew the Skyhawks out of Rio Grande Air Force Base a few hundred miles away, down toward the tip of South America in Tierra Del Fuego. By the time the war finally ended, their Air Force lost most of their fleet, twenty-two Skyhawks in total, many at the hands of British Sea Harriers and ship launched surface to air missiles.

I remember seeing those dogfights. The images from down in my shell scrape are burned into my memory. Those air battles were exciting enough to rouse my attention. Sidewinder missiles launching, huge explosions in the sky, rousing cheers as the Skyhawk plummeted back down to earth. When one of theirs went up in flames, for that brief moment, I could forget my frozen condition and stand up and cheer.

I think everyone huddled up on that beach would agree. Whenever an Argentinean jet managed to get over top of our position, an air red signal was called. Shore positioned anti-aircraft guns located and fired; I too would come running up out of my shell scrape, GPMG over my shoulder, hopeful of squeezing off a shot in time to take down the fast moving intruder. Just as was the case aboard the Canberra though, I never seemed to find the right position to shoot one down. I would fire at what I saw, but in the blink of an eye, the plane would be gone.

On the evening of May 25th, the Argentinean Air Force finally scored a decent hit. Two of their Super Etendard aircraft, equipped with precision, anti-ship Exocet missiles, struck the port quarter of the SS Atlantic Conveyor, where the fuel and ammo were stored. Whether the missiles exploded on impact or after penetrating the hull, no one knows, but once the cargo ignited, the ship exploded into a hellacious inferno.

The next day, crews boarded the Atlantic Conveyor in a vain attempt to salvage whatever they could. There was nothing left though, only smoking rubble and bodies.

Before the ship went down a few days later in tow, the lives of twelve British sailors had been lost, including the ship's master, Captain Ian North.

The sinking of the SS Atlantic Conveyor was one the most damaging incidents suffered by the British military in the entire war.

Even worse, all the Chinook helicopters but one had been destroyed. This meant that British soldiers could no longer count on transport.

We would be forced to yomp from place to place from now on.

At night, fires were forbidden. By daylight though, we were finally allowed to prepare a hot ration. If the weather was not going to cooperate, at least we could warm up our insides. Down in our shell scrape, Gaz and I would light our little fires and cook rations like cave men. Military issue mutton may not be much of a treat, but it is considerably more appetizing when it's served warm.

Over those couple of days on the beach, we also got a chance to refresh our personal supplies. Incoming soldiers carried dry cigarettes. We were able to beg or barter with them for fresh smokes, which most of us had run out of days before.

Like a hot meal, the small comfort of a cigarette goes a long way.

Most of my waking time was spent doing whatever I could to get warm. However hard I tried, I never managed to achieve that objective though.

All of the clothing on my body and in my bag had been soaked through, and consequently, I was chilled down to the bone. Somehow, between relentless cold and wind, I managed to stay as wet as I was when I first made landfall days ago.

Complaining gets a grunt like me nowhere. I knew the rest of the lads were cold as well, but on that beach, I began to realize that my situation was in dire straits.

Trench foot had started to set in. A condition that had been endemic during World War One and the awful warfare that gave it its name, a soldier contracts trench foot from prolonged exposure to damp and unsanitary conditions. Once I settled back on Green Beach, my feet became more than just uncomfortable.

They began to swell up. The nerves were damaged. They started to stink something fierce through the leather, an early sign of necrosis.

For a while, I did my best to keep this reality to myself, though the constant discomfort became unbearable pain. When I took my boots off, I could see my toes were turning unsightly colors, red and blue and even black. Sometimes, my feet would throb, while other times, I lost feeling in them altogether.

I had two pairs of socks in my pack. I kept one pair on my feet and another tucked under my armpits in the vain hope of drying them out. Whenever I had time, I would rotate my socks. I would take my boots off and apply talcum powder to my feet before swapping wet socks for dry; nothing helped though.

Trench foot persisted. The symptoms got worse in spite of constant effort. I confided in Gaz. Side by side down in the shell scrape, it is difficult to keep that much pain under wraps.

For the time being though, Gaz was the only person I told.

While some of the lads might have welcomed a transport back to the safety of the hospital ship, I wanted no part of it. I was here for adventure.

Damn it, I wanted to fight.

The only thing I could do was keep my boots laced up tight. This prevented my feet from swelling up too badly; once my boots were off, my feet ballooned to an uncomfortable size. Once I figured this out, I slept in my boots.

Anything to keep the swelling down; boots on and movement were what I needed. Gratefully, after a couple of long days, we finally received new orders.

Chapter 11
Goose Green

The early stages of the Falkland Island War had been marked by a few firefights and skirmishes. It was not until Sunday, May 23rd, when HQ decided to launch a battalion raid on Goose Green, that combat took on the feel of a full-scale operation.

A tiny sheep farming settlement, Goose Green was located along a central spit of land that was one mile wide and five miles long, about twenty kilometers south of our position back on San Carlos. The narrow isthmus connects Lafonia and Wickham Heights, the two-lobed landmasses that connect the north and south portions of East Falkland Island. Although a considerable Argentinean force had held the village, and its neighboring settlement, Darwin, since early April, an initial strategic assessment said that Goose Green held little value as a military target. As time wore on after our landing, though, British HQ saw capturing the area along Darwin isthmus as a means of encircling the city of Stanley, where most of the enemy forces were located.

It was 2 Para that got the call. By Wednesday the 26th, five hundred troops from that battalion had already moved south.

A few days later, our paratroopers were in position. They were prepared to engage. Combat would come that night against a largely unknown Argentinean force.

Then word came down to our section. We would move out too. Also, 2 Para Company had mounted their full-scale attack to take back Goose Green and Darwin.

On the night of May 28th, we were shipped off in support of 2 Para. Once again, Lou gave us orders. We were only supposed to take our combat order.

A military chopper carried our section over those twenty kilometers into battle. As we approached the isthmus and saw the villages on the horizon, we got a clear view of what was happening on the ground. There was a great deal of intense fighting taking place in a very small area. Machine gun and artillery fire from both sides lit up the gray, cloudy sky. We couldn't hear anything except from a few kilometers out, but high up in the air, we could see the red tracers streaking and explosions of white phosphorous popping off here and there. Lanterns shot straight into the sky. For a brief moment, you could see the whole battlefield below, men racing about, taking shots and hiding out.

We placed on the ground in a support position on the north end of the isthmus. Every staged attack has a start line where forces begin and behind which operations remain in place; we were in back of that line. Again, even from a fair distance, we had a pretty decent view of the fierce fighting taking place down at Goose Green.

HQ had to know that there would be some degree of difficulty in gaining any momentum on the battlefield at Goose Green; perhaps they were counting on sheer military superiority to win the battle, because the circumstances were not in our favor. Battalion 2 Para had been tasked with taking two villages. In order to do so, they had to advance against a force of unknown strength and number, which had been dug in for some time, and they would need to cover a lot of uncovered ground just to get there.

Consequently, there had been a push and pull aspect to combat throughout the first morning of the battle. By mid-day, however, 2 Para had finally broken through. They had softened and pushed the Argentinean lines of defense. British forces were able to advance closer to Darwin and Goose Green, securing strategic hamlets, houses, and farms along their path to victory; on the other side of the isthmus, the Argentineans had started bringing in their re-enforcements. They ran constant support missions from the south. From our position, we could see their choppers approaching in the distance. When quiet flooded back, we could hear the faint, rhythmic thump of rotors in the air.

By that evening, Argentinean forces had squeezed back toward Goose Green. Fighting intensified. Our section, part of J Company of 42 Commando, had arrived on the scene too late to take an active role in the fighting. All that foolish pride Gaz and I and the others had amassed over the last couple of months since April, after seeing the first firefight on the Falklands, evaporated quickly into the smoky air over Goose Green.

It was the lads from 2 Para who were in the teeth of the first real battle.

We had been ordered to bring in a new supply to our rear positioned artillery. After a day of nearly constant shelling, they were coming close to the last of their ordinance; over a stretch of flat ground such as this one, an advancing force needs quite a bit of artillery support. Instead of jumping into the skirmish, our section was given orders to bring them a new supply, and we carried two thirty-pound shells per person in a pack slung over our backs. Our section, which had seen all that glory not too long ago, had been reduced to a pack of highly explosive mules, lugging bombs into combat before we were to retreat back out into support.

On our single file retreat through the darkness, word got passed back.

"Stop," the man in front of me said. "We're in a mine field."

Everyone froze. I staggered, wondering if I'd heard him correctly.

As we fumbled about in the cold, wondering what the hell to do, Lou shouted out an order. We were to continue our retreat, only now back through our old footsteps.

What a load of shit, I thought. They cannot be serious.

I could hardly see the ground two meters out in front of my feet. Now I was supposed go back over where my feet landed in the bog hours ago?

One foot gingerly in front of the other, we continued back toward the start line. Whether or not I could see my old footsteps, I could see where the lad in front of me had stepped.

If he didn't blow up, stands to reason I would not.

Everyone held their breath. We listened with grim expectation that this would be the step when we would hear the click and boom of an exploded mine.

It took two hours for us to get back through the gorse and brackish bog water. We were extremely lucky that no one had lost a leg, or worse.

I spent the rest of that night lying face down in a heap of tussock grass. I kept the GPMG close to my body, hopeful of pulling even a little heat off of it.

The steel was cold to the touch though. It would remain that way unless I were to get the chance to rattle off a few shots, but who knew when that would be.

My teeth rattled. A shiver raced through my damp body, as violent as a seizure. That night, I swear I nearly went down with exposure.

Back near the start line, things were quiet. I dozed off now and then. A thousand meters ahead, there was a battle going on, but we were barely part of it. Even as we got bits of intelligence from the front, good news, there was an air of loneliness.

A few hundred meters away from our position, the Darwin schoolhouse, half way between settlements, went up, exploding into flames like a dry torch. A billow of thick black smoke hung into the sky, and combatants raced around the grounds. The old wood building was the scene of a fierce clash between C and D Companies and retreating Argentinean units after being routed off of nearby Darwin Heights.

One by one, positions south of the start line fell. Momentarily lost control of Darwin Heights was regained, including the regional airstrip. Our boys pushed to the edge of Goose Green. Even though they had started the battle with guns, numbers, and position, the Argentinean forces were on the run. Battalion 2 Para was routing them out.

By morning of the 29th, roughly twenty-four hours after the start of battle, their army had been driven from most of their positions around the village.

They were on the run with their backs against the wall.

The 2 Para battalion raid against Goose Green had been

quite the bold move. When the fighting was finally over and everything sorted out, what we had suspected bore out as truth. The Paratroopers had been significantly outnumbered and badly outgunned. As light came up and we moved out from behind the start line, we could see that in order for our forces to retake the village, they had been forced to charge across flat, open ground under a heavy hail of fire.

Although the lads of 2 Para were our sworn rivals, there was no denying it—that night on the Darwin isthmus, they did one hell of a job.

Lou gave the order—we were to march into Goose Green. As we trudged down that dirt road, we were witness to the battle's grim aftermath. We heard faint groans from the wounded and dying all around. A layer of smoke hung in the sky, lingering over burning buildings and smoldering wreckage. There were helmets and weapons littering the fields all around the village. Some of it was ours. More though, was there's.

There was a helicopter that had exploded. I remember it clearly, walking past and seeing an arm sticking out of a jacket, blown clean off of the body.

As we walked into Goose Green, we saw another line approaching us. When they got closer, we recognized them as some of the nine hundred and fifty Argentinean soldiers that had surrendered during the fight, filtering out past us.

No one said much. Their faces were somber, colored with shame. I didn't bother to look back over my shoulder to see where they were being led.

I remember there were bodies too. Many of the Argentinean dead had been stacked on the roadside, neatly like cordwood. I had never seen a dead body before, at least not up close. Now, all of a sudden, they surrounded me.

Gaz and I walked side-by-side. We were numb from the wet, cold conditions. The lack of sleep had worn me down to a nub. Maybe we were in shock at the grisly sight of all those dead.

Closer in toward town, Gaz got one of his bright ideas. He saw a gold ring on the finger of one of the dead Argentinean soldiers.

"Would you take a look at that?" he said, jokingly. "I'm having that."

Turns out though, he wasn't joking at all. Hungry for a taste of the spoils of war, Gaz placed one foot on the dead man's wrist and leaned over to take it off.

As though coming back from the dead, suddenly the hand curled up. Although it was only tendons recoiling under the weight of his boot, it scared Gaz pretty good.

"Fuck that," he shouted, jumping out of his skin.

He almost shit himself and scattered back into line and kept quiet the rest of the march in. Of course, I got a pretty good laugh out of it as he tried to play it cool.

From what I can recall of Goose Green, it wasn't much at all. We marched into a ghost town consisting of a few farmhouses, a store, and scattered farm buildings. There was a community hall and a flagpole in the middle, with a few dirt roads leading in and out of the town square.

Again, not much to speak of, but we had taken it back.

Combat aftermath requires quite a lot of sorting. After all, war presses onward, and there is no use in leaving a mess behind.

Argentinean prisoners were led out of town to join the others. A new command was set up and communication with HQ established. All the brass put their heads together, figuring out who will go where next.

Of course, we drew the short straw and got the privilege of more heavy lifting. As it turns out, grunt work ended up being J Company's legacy at Goose Green.

Lou tasked us with piling weapons and ammunition that had been seized from all the dead and captured. For the first time in quite a while, the sun came out. I swear to God that was one of the few moments I can recall from those long Falkland Island days where I could actually turn my face to the sky and bask.

When we were done, I remember dozing off. The village was over one shoulder. An open field was over the other.

For the briefest moment, I felt tranquil. I could have been at home.

Then I heard an explosion, loud enough to remind me where I was. Only a split second later, I saw two bodies fly straight up in the air and back down again.

With a gobsmacked look on my face, I looked over at Gaz, who was over a fire.

"Did you see that?"

Only briefly, my mate looked up from his cup of tea and shrugged.

"Did I see what?"

Then he turned back to finish his tea.

Had I been the only one to see that happen? War does that, makes you question. As I recall that moment though, it was like that bloody scene from "Blazing Saddles."

With our support, the Paras had scored a decisive victory at Goose Green. Even though it was by any estimation a rout, it did not come entirely without loss.

Out of the nearly seven hundred British troops who took back the villages, eighteen men had been killed; another sixty-four had been badly wounded.

Throughout the day on May 29th, wounded men were evacuated by helicopter to a hospital ship positioned off shore, the Uganda; those eighteen dead soldiers though, sixteen lads from 2 Paratrooper, one Royal Marine pilot, and one commando sapper, were gathered up in the aftermath and buried in a mass grave a short distance away, out at nearby Ajax Bay, marked only by a square of white stone.

Of those sixteen men, 2 Para also lost one of its commanding officers as well.

It was not long after the battle of Goose Green ended that we all learned the fate of Herbert Jones. A decorated Lieutenant Colonel with over twenty years in the Army and extensive fighting experience in the ongoing Operation Banner to secure Northern Ireland, Jones was killed in combat that night. At 0230 in a torrential downpour of rain, Jones led a multi-pronged attack on Argentinean base positions around Darwin Hill, followed by an isolated settlement, Boca House. Though his battalion was under heavy fire by MAG machine guns and FAL automatic rifles, Jones decided to press onward.

As Major Chris Keeble recalled, Jones spoke bravely.

"Christ, I have waited twenty-two years for this," he said to his second in command. "I am not waiting any longer."

By 0400, his men had gallantly overtaken those objectives, which were critical to victory. Yet it was there, in those small hours, that Jones made another decision, a fateful one that would ultimately cost him his life.

Jones called off an immediate, deeper assault. For all of the nighttime courage, by morning light he had become fearful of leading his weary men in an unbalanced formation against entrenched Argentinean units.

As dawn broke and a flood of battlefield intelligence came in, Jones realized that his decision to delay was proving to be a strategic error; it was then that he opted to lead another assault, full frontal up Darwin Hill, through a rock gully deep and thick with gorse and tussock grass. Trapped on either side, the second Battalion made for easy targets. The Argentinean forces fired on them from above, picking them off with ease until Jones turned around and led a charge against a manned trench from the rear.

A few lads from the second Battalion were wounded in the attack; some did not make it out of the gully. Jones was one of them. He was cut down by a burst of machine gun fire, trying to set things right with what had been, from the start, a bad decision.

The charge was a courageous move, one that falls easily into military legend. Soon afterward, the entrenched Argentinean unit surrendered.

By sun up, 2 Para had taken Darwin Hill, but Jones paid dearly. He had only celebrated his forty-second birthday two weeks before.

I hardly knew Colonel Herbert Jones. He wasn't my commander. But somehow, in the end, his story is so entangled that it has become a small part of mine.

I don't have pictures of him, nor is his image burned in my memory when I think back of my time in the Falklands.

An Internet search yields hits though, his military portraits and a few snap shots of him in the field. He had an affable smile, the kind of guy you could share a pint with.

Later on, after the war was over, Margaret Thatcher lauded the slain commander. In speeches, the Prime Minister often referred to Colonel Jones' death as a turning point. She said that without his sacrifice, the outcome at Goose Green could have turned out much differently. The battle could have gone on much longer, at a steeper cost of life. He was awarded a posthumous Victoria Cross for his courage in battle.

It is tradition that a body is buried close to the place where they fell in battle. Graves are dug wherever is convenient, men disposed of.

After the Falkland Island War was finally over, a few of the bodies buried that morning in their mass grave at Ajax Bay were exhumed and moved to a new location, Blue Beach Military Cemetery at San Carlos, near where we made our first landing. In total, sixteen men took the posthumous journey across the island to their resting place; Jones' body was among those, placed ceremoniously underneath a handsome monument bearing a few solemn words of poetry.

"He is not the beginning but the continuing of the same unto the end."

Now there is a street in Stanley that bears the Colonel's name; you can also take Jones Avenue through Mount Pleasant Air Force Base, also on the Falklands.

Back home in London, Herbert Jones is memorialized as a fallen member of the South Atlantic Task Force in the heart of St. Paul's Cathedral. He is canonized at the Parachute

Memorial at regiment headquarters in Aldershot; the cloisters at Eton and a plaque at Kingswear, in Devon, these too bear his name, etched forever in stone.

If one was so inclined, they could take a small tour across the British countryside of plaques and remembrances in honor of Colonel Herbert Jones.

Herbert's young widow, Sara Jones, was awarded Commander of the Order of the British Empire for her charity work with military causes. Since 2003, she has served as a Deputy Lieutenant of Wiltshire.

The Colonel's sons, Rupert and David, mere children at the time, grew up to serve as infantry reserve officers in the Devon and Dorsets, what has today merged into the Rifles. In 2012, Rupert took command of the First Merchandised Brigade and held that position for two years. He was the youngest in the British Army at the time.

As a curious sort of footnote to Jones' obituary, I remember speaking with a field medic while we were sorting out the aftermath of Goose Green. A few of us were gathered around, and he told us that he had seen Jones' body, and claimed that the entry wound had curiously gone in below his ass; the exit wound blew out of his chest.

It was a gruesome sight to envision, but it left me to wonder—had Colonel Jones been shot while lying down? Or was he on his feet?

Some thirty years later, Osvaldo Olmos, the Argentinean corporal in charge of that trench, recalled seeing Jones charge through alone, leaving his followers behind. Olmos was astonished, for one at the Colonel's bravery, but also at his recklessness, and it may have been his shots, fired from behind, that took Jones down.

In death, Jones became a hero, a symbol of gallantry in warfare. On that bitter morning, though, our eyes were focused forward on the next battle.

Chapter 12
On to Challenger

After the smoke from the battle of Goose Green had cleared away, there were no longer questions regarding the superiority of an organized British military force. Even the Argentinean junta had to recognize that their best men were on the run, their precarious hold on the islands suddenly in peril. In the days leading up to landfall, they had been hopeful of an indifferent response; what they ended up getting was a war.

Seemed like almost everyone took a souvenir of one kind away from the battle. We called it "proffing," a word you likely won't find in any dictionary. Proffing means taking the spoils of war. Gaz tried for that gold ring and almost shit himself. Some guys picked up Argentinean knives, others snatched a pistol or left-behind machine gun.

What did I take? I proffed a metal mug for my souvenir. Humble as it may be, the way I figured, I already had a gun, and a damn impressive one at that.

With a metal mug, I could boil water to make tea.

One hundred and twelve Falkland citizens had been imprisoned in the village community hall at Goose Green; most of them had been cooped up in there for more than a month by the time we freed them. On the evening after the battle, we moved in there, out of the rain. We were all weary and badly sleep deprived. Our company piled into the single-room building only to find a hardwood dance floor and little more than a few tables and chairs for our accommodations. Only a few hours earlier, this place was a military prison; now it would serve as our makeshift barracks.

The roof was still intact. Enclosed in four solid walls, the community hall was decent shelter out of the wind, and it was warm. Yet as welcome as a heated room sounded when offered, the sudden exposure to warmth wreaked havoc on my body. The pain in my feet, already bad, became quickly out of control.

My body became weak and my limbs fell limp. I tumbled down onto a place on the floor near where Gaz was curled up, riddled with the heat aches, an extreme symptom of hypothermia. A disorienting feeling overtook me. I became badly nauseous and my muscles cramped up. A severe headache pulsed as I tried to tough it out.

I pulled off my boots. As quick as I could, I swapped my wet socks out for dry ones. I massaged my toes. I gave them a quick dose of talcum powder. I allowed my feet to breathe, hopeful of finding any measure of relief. Nothing worked though.

Night fell. Outside in the village, things got quiet. Inside, the community hall was pitch black. Soldiers slept any-where they could. They lay with their backs to the wall, up on tables, or curled into corners underneath them. No one had a sleeping bag to slip into yet, so instead, we found comfort in whatever we could find in our fighting order, cobbling together a pillow or blanket that we could sleep on.

Although we were for the moment safe, the scene ended up being chaotic. Since we were under the cover of a roof, we were allowed to make a cook fire. Most of the soldiers fixed a proper cup of tea and their first hot meal in days. I remember the constant sound of voices. Men shouted through the night, back and forth to one another, telling battle stories, anything it seemed besides sleep, to fill the time.

My feet throbbed so terribly that I could hardly stand it. I can still remember that feeling now; it was awful. I vividly remember the feeling. It was like someone sticking hot needles into my feet. When you hurt that badly, it is difficult to put it out of mind.

Over and over, I tried to find any relief. I took my wet boots off. I would cover my feet in another coating of fresh powder, then I would again dig the dry socks out of their stash under my armpits to replace the wet ones.

This was supposed to work, but when I put my socks back on and placed my boots over them, my feet throbbed worse than before.

I rolled over and woke up Danny, who was fast asleep beside me.

"Danny, Danny," I said.

"Huh?"

"I'm fucked, I'm fucked," I ranted.

I showed him my feet. All he could do was shrug and eye me drowsily.

"Suck it up," he said, then rolled back to sleep. "What do you want me to do about your bloody feet?"

I didn't want to hear that. Of course, Danny was right.

Though my feet were absolutely fucked, I had no choice but to suck it up and deal with the pain. Outside of the community hall there were shell-shocked men with real combat wounds, bullet holes, broken and missing limbs.

My sodden feet hardly registered.

With throbbing feet and hot aches as bad as I had ever known before, I tried to sack out. Though I was beyond exhaustion, I simply couldn't sleep.

That night on the floor of the Goose Green Community Hall was one of the longest of my entire life, until that point or since.

The next morning, we woke before dawn. As I came out for formation, my feet still hurt badly. Somehow though, I had found the means to endure the pain.

We made a spot of tea in the square. We prepared and ate whatever food we had. When we were done, we were ordered to queue up, and Lou gave us the order: We would be leaving Goose Green.

I remember trudging back out of the village the same way we came in. That was a quiet morning, reflective. My mind was riddled with questions though.

Where were we going next? Were the Islanders simply going to put their lives and homes back together now?

By mid-morning, all of the Argentinean prisoners were gone. Where they had been taken, I didn't know. But the field was still strewn with the litter of battle. There was no one there though. Only the ghosts of Goose Green remained.

The bodies of the Argentinean dead had yet to be removed from the roadside. We could see them stacked up from a hundred meters away, like cords of twisted, rotten firewood. As we got closer, my pace slowed. The foul stink of death lingered heavily around the corpses; so strong that you dreaded your next breath.

As I trudged past, I looked around for the hand. I wanted to give Gaz a good jab about the gold ring. Then I found it, curling stiff and dangling out on the dirt road.

This time though, the gold ring was gone. And whoever claimed that prize ended up having to cut the whole damn finger off in order to get it.

An air of anticipation hung over 42 Commando as we lined up a few kilometers down the road from Goose Green. Our next stop was the battlefront in the area of Mount Kent, but for the moment, where we were going hardly seemed a relevant topic. How we were getting there did, however. No one had ridden in a Chinook Helicopter before, but that's what we were told was coming. We chattered on about the privilege. Anything for a little excitement, I suppose.

We heard the engine roar and rotors chop before the massive helicopter circled down out of the thick clouds. The aircraft settled onto the field and the doors flew open. The loadmaster leaned out and took a quick look at the lot of us charging at him.

"What the fuck is this?" he shouted, throwing his hands in the air furiously. "There are too damn many of you!"

He stuck up his fingers, indicating how many men he could take with him. We quickly learned that a Chinook helicopter, however massive it seemed, only carries about fifty-five fully dressed soldiers. That total was about half of 42 Commando. We ducked back out of the rotor chop and stood around waiting as command sorted things.

After what felt like hours, it was finally decided. 45 Commando would be the poor blokes staying back. They would yomp half way to hell to the fight at Mount Kent, while the rest got to hop on board and take the ride.

I don't know who in command fucked up, but it felt like amateur hour. In hindsight, I wonder, was even a simple head count above their pay grade?

In the moment, all I cared about was to say thanks to whoever negotiated transportation. As I climbed up on board that chopper, I was bloody grateful that our section was getting the ride. I certainly did not want to yomp across the island again, or worse yet, get left hanging around Goose Green, cleaning up the mess that had been left behind.

A Chinook helicopter is everything it's cracked up to be. What an impressive machine. I remember the feeling of being lifted straight up off the ground. Looking down as we soared away, I could see the eyes of those lads who were left behind. They watched enviously as we circled out over the Choiseul Sound before cutting out on northern course into a bank of low settled clouds.

I couldn't see anything on the ground once we were really moving. Of course, on the Falkland Islands, there isn't much of a landscape to see besides one grassy hill after another, another rolling meadow and so on. During that ride, all I caught was a deafening ear full of rotor noise and a fog streaming out in front of our chopper.

Eventually, the chopper began to slow down. The pilots prepared for landing. We were nearing our destination, although no one could see anything up ahead in the mist, let alone a bloody mountaintop. Those Marines on the outside row craned their necks in an attempt to get a quick view as we felt the vehicle lower toward the ground.

Everyone grabbed their fighting order and held on tight. We were mere inches from the ground before we saw the grass.

Because of the terrible noise, orders in a chopper are given in a series of hand signals. Major Mike Norman looked back from his seat and gave 42 Commando a go. One by one, we jumped out of the cabin and fell into our defensive position, forming a protective circle around the hovering chopper as the Boss got out and situated. Then, as quick as the chopper landed, it prepared for lift off again.

That mountaintop was eerie. I could hardly find the business end of my GPMG two feet in front of me on account of the fog being so dense. Gaz was the next guy over, somewhere close by my side, but I could see neither hide nor hair of him.

It was like I was suddenly alone. For a fleeting moment, it felt to me like there was not another soul anywhere on our mountaintop.

As the Chinook vanished back into the clouds and the sound of its chirping whirling blades gradually dissipated, we wrapped back into the silence of nature. It got so damn quiet so fast that you could hear the quick breath coming from the guy next to you.

Had the Chinook dropped us at Mount Kent?

Or were we on the wrong hill altogether? We all wondered, because this certainly didn't feel like the scene of a military operation.

If a head count was out of the question, could command read a bloody map?

As hours passed, it became painfully clear that the Boss didn't have a clue where we had been put down. We struggled to orient ourselves. There were no visible reference points to gauge our location, so Lou told us to listen for any bursts of artillery fire from down in the valleys below our position.

The logic was, if we heard something, perhaps voices, we could figure out where the hell the enemy was positioned.

We followed orders, which was our lot in life. We staggered out into our positions, where we manned our customary arcs of fire. As we were told, we listened for an enemy below that we had no chance of catching a glimpse of.

There was still only silence, and that felt like bloody madness.

The lads in 42 Commando ended up spending one night alone atop that mountain. We were helplessly exposed to a frozen fog, confronted with a cold that penetrated our wet, thin uniforms like a frozen lance.

I was miserable. The relentless throbbing began in my feet again. My face burned from the constant wind. We were without food and tea; the last of our rations had been eaten back at the community hall in Goose Green. We searched far and wide, but there was no fresh water anywhere to be found.

Gaz and I shared a few coarse words. What could you do but endure though? The Bergens containing our bloody sleeping bags were down below, probably at San Carlos. What I wouldn't do to crawl back into that shell scrape.

As night pressed, the worst part of our ordeal became the element of the unknown. No one knew where the hell we were, regardless of where artillery fire was located. Our enemies surrounded us, but we had no means of locating them. We had been on this awful island for what felt like forever and not fired a single shot yet.

At Goose Green, we had been packed up like artillery mules. As I tried desperately to fall asleep up on that terrible mountain, I felt like a first class ass.

Blessings on the Falklands came not from the moments of stillness but rather they arrived in our collective movement. Too much time spent idle plays havoc on a Marine's imagination, and by now my feet were so fucked, I had to keep walking.

The next day, we got our order from HQ: Time to go. They had discovered the location of the rest of our unit, across the valley on top of Wall Mountain. The prevailing sentiment amongst the other Marines wasn't tough to figure out. Thank bloody God, let's go.

We were sent down the mountainside. Major Mike Norman spread us into a formation and we plunged downward, head first, blindly into the teeth of that fog. If it were even possible, the air around us seemed thicker on that morning than the previous day.

Blind and in the dark, we were used to that now.

Anyone who runs in a marathon will agree; the toughest leg on the body is going down the hill, not up. Descending the steep hillside in those conditions was precarious, and beat our already sore, aching bodies to hell. We stumbled over rocky ground, through thickets of damn tussock grass; memories of which still haunt me to this day. Moving without incident was impossible, but hours later, we reached a narrow valley.

Where would we go next? Without hesitation, Major Mike

Norman ordered us to yomp back up the next steep face, onto Wall Mountain. Up, down and up and down. We felt like a bunch of yo-yos, dangling in the hands of children. I was beaten down with exhaustion. Only the prospect of a welcome sea of familiar faces greeting us hastened my step.

We all held our breath as we reached that summit, a rock pile similar to the last. A measure of doubt had crept in on us. HQ had put us on top of the wrong bloody mountain once already, after all. Who is to say we were where we were supposed to be?

Fortunately, our gnawing sense of anxiety would not end up being warranted. The rest of our unit was indeed positioned up there on the summit of Wall Mountain, anticipating our arrival from across the valley. As we trudged back on and assimilated into the group, I must admit that it felt pretty damn good to get a load of their shit.

"Yeah, yeah, we were lost mate. Now get me a cup of tea, I'm freezing!"

There isn't much variety on the Falkland Islands. The only difference between one hill and the next was a matter of orders, and ultimately, its proximity to Stanley.

Wall Mountain was just as cold, just as foggy and just as bleak. The difference was, we were supposed to be up here. Purpose doesn't keep you warm; it does, however, give you a more compelling story to share over tea while you're waiting for the next shoe to drop, which for lads like us, would likely come on a moment's notice.

For better or worse, Gaz was my shadow in those days, and I was his. A mate like that brings comfort in the military, a rock you can lean on. We were inseparable. Got to the point up there where we could finish one another's sentences.

Our sleeping bags were waiting for us. There was ample space up on Wall Mountain to set up a two-man camp, and Gaz found a suitable place for ours. From time to time, we even got a few moments to sack out. With fresh rations and lukewarm back tea in our bellies, we began to feel human again, like we were getting somewhere.

That rejuvenated feeling was, however, a short lived one. Even a returned sleeping bag can't prevent an erosion of morale like we experienced on Wall Mountain.

Those were some of the longest days in my military career.

We may have had our sleeping bags back, but we didn't have tents. What we had been given by command to use as rain cover were these ponchos; thin nylon sheets—like flimsy green tarps—that we were supposed to stretch out and tie down over our sleeping bags. That was supposed to provide our cover.

Gaz and I took one look at the poncho they handed us and scoffed. Maybe for a sunny spring afternoon in the park, we thought. This was the Falklands though.

Our little camps were affectionately referred to as "bivvies", and each and every bivvie on Wall Mountain had one thing in common—the ponchos were bloody useless. If a Marine actually managed to tie one of the flimsy plastic sheets down, they were hardly sturdy enough to keep the rain off, especially when it was driving sideways, pounding at all hours. In those blustery Falkland winds, without solid earth to hammer a stake into, the flaps would frequently fly up. One of the sleeping Marines would have to get up and try and restake the thing down in order to keep it from blowing away.

Imagine sleeping outside in the worst bloody storm you've

ever endured. Now imagine trying to do so without a sleeping bag, underneath nothing but a rain fly.

The lack of proper cover was an aggravation. We had choice words. It was not very long, though, before our sleeping conditions began to take on near dire consequences.

One night, Danny and his bivvie mate lost their poncho in the relentless wind. That was the middle of the night, one of the coldest, wettest we had endured on the Falkland Islands. With the swirling winds howling so hard and fierce, their poncho, stakes probably wedged between stones, flew away. Before either one of the lads could turn around and try to fetch it, the bloody thing was probably a hundred meters away; maybe it was all the way down in the valley somewhere.

Where that useless piece of plastic ended up hardly bloody mattered. What mattered to Danny and his bivvie mate was that they were in the open without any cover. The wind was so fierce that you could hardly hear a thing above its savage howl. If Danny had been outside, screaming for help, it was unlikely anyone would hear him.

The rule of "every man for himself" applies in moments like that one. In a frozen panic, surely his mate scurried off and found shelter under someone else's poncho, leaving Danny out to fend for himself. With the cold and rain relentless, unable to sleep or stay dry in the open, he moved across the hilltop, searching for any place he could cover up. After being unable to find space under anyone's poncho, Danny was forced up a ways from the main camp, where he sought shelter in the bivvie of a Corporal, one of the unit's commanders.

Officers were granted the first choice of where to set up

their camp. Call this one of the advantages of rank: a prime choice in your sleeping arrangements. The lucky bastard chose a sheltered crevasse; already half way out of the rain, he found one of the best places up on Wall Mountain to set up his sleeping poncho.

Regardless of the wind, his cover wasn't going anywhere.

With nowhere else to go, Danny dove into the Corporal's bivvie. The NCO (Non-Commissioned officer) was startled to find that he was no longer alone. Soaking wet and pathetic, half frozen by wind, Danny begged him to please, let him stay.

The Corporal denied him. The bastard booted him out of the tent on his own. What an awful lot of shite.

Sometime later that night, deeply shaken and near death from hypothermia, Danny found Gaz and I bagged in our bivvie.

"Let me in, let me in," he said, barely able to speak he was so riddled with shivers. "I'm dying out here."

We hardly had any room to spare. Gaz and I were already wrapped together, but we could not turn him away. One look at the lad and you knew he was in a bad way.

"Aright, aright," Gaz replied. "Get in here."

Danny burrowed down in the rocks. Grateful, he found a place between our bodies and we warmed him up. He was shivering fierce, teeth rattling.

"It's going to be aright," we assured him, over and over.

Danny was on the brink of death that night. I hate to think what would have happened had he not made it under our poncho.

He would have likely died on Wall Mountain, a victim of carelessness.

The next morning, over a cup of tea, Danny told us what had led him to our bivvie. He spilled his guts on everything from the moment the wind took his poncho away, to the smug refusal at the hands of the Corporal. I was aghast hearing that story. The rest of the lads were downright furious. A lot of nasty chatter went around those campsites, until Butch stood up from where he had been listening.

"Let's kill him," Butch said.

No one responded; we didn't know quite how. With those grim words dangling out there, I remember shooting a look over his way. If ever there was an "old sweat" in the Royal Marines, old Butch was that lad. Telling by the steely look in his hard eyes, he was dead fucking serious. Butch had killed men, a countless number, and if he had had boots on his feet that moment, he may have gone and added another to his list right then and there.

We managed to talk Butch down from killing the Corporal that morning. I don't recall how we did it, but somehow, cooler heads prevailed.

In the process, though, one thing became quite clear, at least to me.

The harsh conditions on Mount Wall were burning through our morale. At any moment before, we would have been discrete about threats on a Corporal's life. Now there was open talk of killing one of our leaders.

Everyone was taking a turn down a dark path. Danny would not get over that night. At least, not until weeks later, when he got what we all saw as his revenge.

Gaz and I kept our heads down. We did our best to focus on what we saw as most critical—staying alive until the next order came and saved us from oblivion. However harsh, all we could do was endure the conditions. We had not been forgotten, but until logistics had been set up and orders given, Wall Mountain was our reality.

We had regular duty to keep us occupied. Gaz and I took our customary turn on watch detail. We were sent out daily to a forward position on the mountain, where we would look for any enemy troop movements. Watch is a boring task. Most of the time, the hardest thing is staying awake and alert through your hour.

All Gaz and I had to do was keep our eyes open. We made sure that whatever was rustling the sea of grass around Wall Mountain was only the wind, instead of some Argentinean commando creeping up with a grenade.

Gaz and I spent quite a lot of time out on watch, shooting the shit, talking about whatever there was to talk about. Mostly though, we were quiet, eyes open.

Patrols were sent down to scour the base valley at all times. For what it was worth, Gaz and I preferred going out on patrol to sitting watch. A patrol gave you something to do, a specific thing to look out for. We were sent to particular coordinate locations to see if we could find something. The constant movement was good for my aching feet. Even if you came back from patrol empty handed, the good yomp kept you a hell of a lot warmer than sitting around on a rock, twiddling your thumbs.

As mind numbing as the routine was, it kept us from going completely mad.

There is one patrol that I recall as clear as yesterday.

We were down the hillside, a short distance from the summit. As we moved stealthily across a rippling landscape, we spotted movement just ahead of our position.

As far as we knew, no one was supposed to be there.

Our first call went out to control. We asked if there were any friendly troops operating forward of our location. The reply crackled back:

"No friendly troops forward of your position."

They advanced toward us. We could see their heads, a hundred meters ahead. Still, we couldn't make out any detail.

My finger went to the trigger.

"Can you confirm, please?"

"No friendly troops forward of your position...."

I watched as they even drew closer. I was ready to fire. I was about to squeeze off a shot when the radio came back again.

"Friendly troops in your area of operation."

I breathed a sigh of relief and lowered my gun. Our patrol went out to greet a couple of lads from the 148 Forward Observation Battery, an elite unit, carefully selected for their commando skills, as well as their ability to spot and call for enemy fire.

Lucky for us, we got word in time, or they would have been cut down.

The day in, day out on Wall Mountain remained bleak. After an hour's watch and a short patrol, there was still a lot of day to kill.

The weather was relentless. We were a few days in and there still weren't any dry cigarettes to cool our nerves with. My body only got wetter and the condition of my trench foot worsened. Days had passed since we'd received any new rations or clean water.

Out of desperation, some Marines took to drinking bog water. Those lads got a care of the shits something fierce for it too. We heard stories about soldiers toward the latter days of the war who had diarrhea so bad that they cut the seat out of their pants because it got so damn tedious pulling them down every ten minutes. It was one less step before relief. I'll bet those stories never made it home to warm, cozy London on the evening news.

We got so batty at one point, we started calling out the name of the hospital ship, "Uganda, Uganda." Any time anyone nicked their finger, or coughed, someone would bellow those words.

"Uganda, Uganda. Come rescue me from this awful hell."

One Marine was so desperate to get off the mountain that he crippled himself with a shovel. He took a swing at his kneecap and almost took it clean off. Quite a sight, I'm sure.

I don't know the lad. He wasn't in our section, but we heard the story. That Marine got a med-evac off of Wall Mountain to the Uganda for his deed; a helicopter ride and a bloody lot of shite from the rest of us. We all wanted off that rock, but it was seen as a low, cowardly move to try and force it.

There isn't a whole lot of glory in warfare. Glory is for the bloody movies.

Chapter 13
Mount Harriet

After surviving almost ten long days up on Wall Mountain, we finally received our move orders. It was the morning of June 11th when we were sent back out to the battlefield. This time, our objective was to take Mount Harriet.

The position was fortified, which meant we would be in for a firefight. A little combat action sounded inviting, at least compared to spending another uncertain night fighting each other atop that God forsaken rock. Better to take your shots at the enemy than each other, the way I saw things. We were restless. We needed to engage.

Mount Harriet sits at the center of a chain of mountains and ridges east of Stanley. Taking a look at the battle map now, the clear British plan was to strangle the Argentinean forces once and for all.

Divided into four sections under the command of Lieutenant Colonel Nick Vaux, just a lad then, who would later on become a General, 42 Commando was ordered to make the first of a multi-pronged attack on Mount Harriet from all surrounding ridges. Approximately four hundred well-entrenched Argentinean soldiers in the Fourth Infantry regiment were up defending Harriet, under the command of Diego Soria.

The First Battalion of the Welsh Guards was in charge of securing the start line. Once they accomplished that on the 9th of June, they would hold up there in reserve with two units from 40 Commando. In the water a few miles off shore, the HMS Yarmouth would provide a barrage of naval gunfire support, while both L and K companies would launch up the hill from the line southeast of the target.

J Company remained in position on Wall Mountain. We were roughly one mile due west of Mount Harriet's steep front slope. Rather than jump in from the start line with L and K Companies though, our attack would come later and from the front side. We would rush up the gut, sneaking in while the Argentineans were engaged.

At 20:30, L Company began the initial attack. They would move along the south ridge, up the southwest slope of Mount Harriet, climbing gradually to an elevation of approximately eight hundred meters. As the first unit to reach the mountaintop, their mission would be to draw the Argentinean defenders into a firefight, pulling them out of the safety of their dugout positions. As they took the fight to the defenders, K Company would come up on the northeast edge, around dusk at 21:30, then push beyond Harriet, to engage the Argentinean units further north on a little hill called Goat Ridge.

This was a classic configuration for the military seizure of an elevated defender. Once we held positions on those mountains, we would have a clear ride into town.

We got our fighting order together. An air of excitement pulsed through our ranks as we prepared for our move. Everyone knew that this was going to be one hell of a yomp, covering terrible terrain on our way up to the top of that bloody mountain, but once we were up there, the

Argentineans wouldn't stand a chance. We would have those bastards surrounded on all sides.

We finally got our move order around 0400. As we prepared to move in darkness across the valley, Lou got word from HQ, and he sent it down through the ranks.

"Forward of the start line," he said. "Anyone that is shot or injured, be aware, there will be no med-evacs coming for you."

Holy shit, I thought. We are on our own.

While waiting for the attack, I remember a faint red dot, racing across the inky sky. Perhaps it's a chopper, I thought lazily.

Soon though, everything overhead lit up, and I was struck with a realization. That wasn't a helicopter after all. An Excocet missile had been fired from the island.

The Battle of Mount Harriet had its starting gun.

Within seconds, the whole side of the ridge lit up like a tacky Christmas tree. From where I sat, I could see it all. For a moment, it was glorious.

Then daydreaming was over. It was time to get a move on.

Artillery is an important element to winning a battle; it is especially critical, however, when attacking a mountain by moonlight, like we did that night.

As we ran like a pack of madmen across the flat, rugged terrain, our forward observers called fire back to 29 Commando of the Royal Artillery. Those lads shelled Mount Harriet constantly, laying Argentinean positions to waste with more than three thousand rounds, often fired within one hundred meters of friendly troops.

Precision like that is inspiring.

There was precision and then there was Lou, falling down at least ten times over the course of that yomp. Each time he fell on his face, he bolted back up, just like a child's pop-up toy and continued on.

If I could have taken a moment to laugh at the clumsy sight, I would have.

Once, Lou stopped and turned to face me. As the GPMG carrier, I was up front, close on his heels. I can still see it now. Lou's face was no more than a foot from mine when a hot rush of air and molten shrapnel tore through the air between us.

We were God damn lucky. We came that close, a matter of mere inches, to losing our faces in an airburst explosion.

Getting up that mountain with all twenty-four pounds of that GPMG draped around my neck was an exhausting ordeal, to say the very least. Everyone loves taking a shot with the big gun, but carrying it, you're on your own.

The sun was starting to come up. The atmosphere down at the base of Mount Harriet was thick with smoke and mist. I never looked down at my watch to clock the time, but I remember that it took two hours to get to the top of that hill.

Gaz and I stuck close together. He was second on the GPMG. During that entire climb up the west slope of Mount Harriet, we came under constant defensive fire from Argentinean artillery units, positioned a few kilometers away in Stanley.

As tough as the boggy Falkland terrain is for a yomp, it actually does a good turn of mitigating disaster when it comes to fire. Mortar shells don't explode on impact with a soft, boggy surface; rather, wet earth swallows the shells up whole. Over rocky terrain, or on the asphalt of a city street, even if the impact of an exploding shell misses your body, its hail of hot metal shrapnel will shred the skin right off of your face.

White phosphorous is another story altogether. When one of those bombs explodes, a crisp rain of hot, white spray streaks down through the sky, so hot that it burns clothing and skin on impact. Those detonations leave behind smoke, at first bright enough to light the immediate area, then becoming thick enough to provide cover.

How to survive was clear—as long as those shells struck the bog and not our heads, and we stayed out of the white-hot rain of phosphorous, we would be fine.

Most of the war movies you see get one critical aspect wrong. Through the air, mortar fire is silent. Shells only make a sound when on impact. The thud of the bog water swallowing a mortar shell is quite strange when you hear it for the first time.

A soldier's nerves are steeled for battle; we have no choice. Defenses against loud sounds like gunshots, screams, and explosions are natural; block it out, become numb. The eeriness of combat silence is often more unsettling. When I think back on those moments of silence, they haunt me deeply.

I remember Danny falling down. We were still on our dash up the front of the hillside. If I remember that moment correctly, it was a silent one, a space between explosions and the hellish rains of white phosphorous.

For a tense moment, his body just lay there, sprawled helplessly on the ground. Obviously, I wasn't in the lad's head, so I don't know what got him moving again.

If it had been me that fell though? All I would have needed to do was look around me at all that chaos and remember Lou's words: "No one coming to get you lads."

I remember a lot from that night, but the images are patched together. Keeping those bound together are my adrenaline-fueled emotions.

It is not fear or excitement of battle that sticks with me; rather, it's the exhaustion, down to my core, of body and mind.

Once we were atop Mount Harriet, confusion took over.

We held our collective breath. I was primed for a firefight. I am pretty sure Gaz was as well. Through all of that hellfire getting to the top, we were quite unsure what we would find. And as we crested the hill, we found there was no enemy to engage.

There were no surprises. There was, however, a rain of gunfire from Argentinean defenders. We crossed the plateau through the smoke in silence. It did not take long for us to figure out they were on the opposite side of the hill, engaged with L and K Companies.

This left us a few moments on our own to get our bearings.

It was around 0600. The sun was coming up on the eastern horizon. I was too bloody exhausted from carrying the GPMG to do anything other than secure a decent position, overlooking the ocean.

A fundamental shift took place once we secured that mountaintop. With the bulk of the Argentinean forces chased away, their 155mm guns began offensive fire on us from Stanley; and in turn, our guns shifted to defensive fire.

That first burst of offensive fire didn't last very long; a few minutes, maybe. As it abated, all I could think was that they were running short of ammo, just like we were. Although we had the position, their assault would continue to the bitter end.

We had been on the mountain an hour, and Gaz and I knew we would need cover. Just like on our ascent up the hillside, shells were swallowed up in the spongy bog, splashing a storm of cold water and filth in a wind halo around impact.

We were already wet to the bone. Fucking great, I thought. Now we're going to be wet and filthy with Falkland bog.

Throughout that morning of June 12th, the consequences of the Battle of Mount Harriet were carefully sorted. Argentinean soldiers dropped their weapons and gave up the fight; they streamed past Gaz and I in droves, escorted by Marines.

I don't know where they were taken, but it didn't take long for them to vanish.

Three hundred Argentinean troops threw up their hands and surrendered. It was roughly seventy-five percent of the force that had held the mountain the day before.

Less than two dozen of their soldiers were lost on Mount Harriet. As the light came up though, it felt like we were confronted with the faces of every single one of those poor bastards. Dead and dying men littered the mountaintop.

Gaz and I watched as they passed by. No one said a word. There were no taunts or torment that I heard. These were lads similar to us. They were young and eager soldiers, and they knew that they did not stand a chance against the Royal Marines.

The guys who seized Government House were their elite

commando units. These guys? They were conscripts.

They had been drafted from Argentinean peasantry and they did not want to die. All they wanted was to make it back home.

At least we have that much in common, I thought.

With the main battle all but won, Gaz and I sought a place to sack out and get some rest. On top of Mount Harriet, where the Argentineans had been holed up, was like an abandoned campsite. All we had was a rain fly, so we stumbled into one of their tents. Not only was that tent three walls worth of refuge from the conditions, it came complete with a pair of dry sleeping bags.

We didn't hesitate a second before diving in and claiming one as our own.

Maybe it was brave. Maybe it was out of plain stupidity. I remember being overcome with a sense of relief. There would be no more ponchos, no more makeshift bivvies for us; at least not for a little while. We promptly fell asleep under proper cover.

Gaz and I made out like a pair of bandits in that tent. We picked up a few packs of smokes, which was a nice find. Fresh, dry cigarettes, enough to go around.

The Argentinean rations we scavenged up were a far cry better than our shite. I remember being ravenously hungry, digging into theirs, which came with a few sausages and different spice combinations, good tastes, if for nothing more than variety. Rummaged from the leftovers, we found a bottle of spirits and some chocolate too.

I don't know what we toasted to, but that drink and sweetness were heaven sent. For a few moments, Gaz and I felt almost human.

It's sometimes funny what sticks in my memory, especially as I creep toward my old age. Out of that whole ordeal fighting in the Falklands, few things stay with me more strongly than the feeling of finding a sleeping bag in that Argentinean tent. Red and plush, that bag was stuffed with the softest down.

Most important though, the bag was dry. As my body slid inside, it felt like heaven after spending weeks soaked and freezing.

That was the warmest bag I had ever slept in, so naturally, I took it. And I don't mind saying, that bag went everywhere with me for years after coming home.

A lot of movement happened up on Mount Harriet as we dozed. The activity was not as chaotic as it had been on Mount Wall, but there were troops yomping through, passing our tent all the time.

I remember Gaz was lying down. We had just claimed the tent and he was bagged out, beyond exhaustion.

Carelessly, Gaz let his boots stick out the open tent flap. There they were, out in plain sight for anyone passing by. Although they were our mates, every one of those troops was looking for a little loot, a trophy of some kind to take home.

I don't remember seeing the lad's face. I cannot be sure, but it was likely one of the Welsh Guards passing our tent who took an interest in his shiny black leather.

"Look at these boots," he said, as he leaned over and started tugging.

"Fuck off," Gaz said, waking up to the rude intrusion of someone trying to take his shoes. "These are my boots and I'm not fucking dead yet."

I remember feeling secure in that tent, especially when I was tucked up inside that new bag. Although we knew we were without any real protection from the bombs going off all around us, there was warmth and a rare, sublime feeling.

RAF jets screamed over our heads, high enough to avoid Argentinean radar. They were dropping cluster bombs on targets all around us, but I dozed off.

At one point, I remember having to take a shit so bad that I could not wait. I told Gaz and scurried out of the tent, found a spot, dug a hole and squatted over it.

Gaz looked out at me and says, "You can't go out there."

"What does it matter?" I replied and went about my business.

Can't go here? A bomb could have hit me in the tent just as easily as it could have hit me squatting over that hole.

Maybe there was a dirty halo hanging over my head, the product of delirium. I felt impervious though, safe, as though those bombs couldn't hit me.

As I indulged my animal side, a shell blew off a few yards from me. Immediately, my backside was covered in bog mud.

Gaz got a good chuckle as I came back. "Nice stink," he said.

Surviving the Battle of Mount Harriet, like any other, was a matter of fortune.

Gaz and I could count as a couple of the lucky ones. In one of the rare quiet moments up there, I remember him saying that he had slept with me more than he had with his girlfriend back home.

Bloody lucky guy I was. I wonder if she would have been jealous to hear that.

Our little vacation on top of Mount Harriet would not last forever. Later that day, Gaz and I had to get up for duty.

By the afternoon, our second in command was in camp. He gave a couple of sections a choice between shite duties. One section had to bury dead Argentinean bodies; the other had to leave our mountaintop position and descend a couple of miles down the Stanley side of Mount Harriet to fetch rations.

Burying the bodies was one thing; we knew it had to be done eventually. The second duty didn't quite make sense though. We had gathered up enough Argentinean rations to last a week, longer than we would have to stay in our position.

Lou volunteered our section for the grave-digging job, and that meant it was Jim MacKay's boys that would have to yomp off and pick up the ration drop.

As bad as I felt for them for having to risk their necks, I was grateful that we hadn't been stuck with that duty.

Jim MacKay, Mac as we knew him, came into our tent moments later. He had a worried look on his usually jovial mug.

"John," he said, voice riddled with worry. "Pass something onto my mother?"

"Sure," I said.

"If I don't come back, tell her I was a good boy, would you?"

The old sweat was bloody scared for his life, and with bloody good reason. Without hesitation, I assured him that I would find his Mom, if anything went wrong.

Mac and his guys could see what should have been painfully obvious to anyone. As soon as that section were to descend onto the mountainside, bare of cover, the Argentinean spotters would locate them and guns open fire; they would be easy targets.

Their fears were affirmed. Not ten minutes after they departed camp, silence was broken. One of the big 155mm artillery guns went off from Stanley; it boomed out a few times, then went eerily silent. We held our breath.

I remember nothing except knowing they had been hit.

No more than five minutes later, a lone soldier from that section scampered back up the hill. We knew him as Eggman, and he was flustered. We took him into our tent. Eggman was a nervous sort, but the way we found him, his nerves were shot all the way through; shock had taken over his senses. I remember getting him a hot sweet wet, our slang for a cup of tea, and allowing him a few moments to sort things out.

When he was finally able to put the words together, he told us his section had been hit pretty hard, and he was the only one in the section able to get away.

Someone asked, where are the others?

Where he had left them, Eggman replied, torn to shreds on the mountainside.

As we had been informed the previous morning, Army chopper pilots would not fly forward of the demarcation line to pick up the wounded. We were on our own.

Royal Marine pilots were quite a different story though. Vowing never to leave a single man behind, one pilot flew his chopper into the hot fire of Mount Harriet's east side and fetched whatever survivors he could and transported them to the Uganda.

Talk about courage; choosing loyalty to a fellow Marine above anything else. I never got the chance to meet that pilot, but I have respect for him.

Five men survived that attack. And they all owe their life to one man.

One of those survivors was Mac. He got a hot piece of 155mm Argentinean shell in his neck for following orders.

Thank God I never had to go see his mother. I don't know how I would face her if the story was that her son had died because some Army pilots refused to med-evac, or worse, over an unnecessary errand for supplies not needed.

Burying the bodies was a shit detail as well. Only difference was, a dead Argentinean soldier wasn't going to shoot you like the live ones would.

The soldiers had been dead for a while. By the late afternoon, their bodies had gone stiff with rigor mortis, which meant they were heavy.

There was no easy way to dig a grave into the rocky soil. We made the best of it though. We tossed the bodies down into the crevasses. We covered them with stones, hopeful of keeping buzzards and scavenging animals off. Our section worked quietly, but there was no reverence; we stacked them like cord wood and disposed of them.

When the unit Chaplain came out and asked where the Argentinean dead were, we pointed to the general area. I watched him walk out. He quickly crossed himself and offered a few hushed words. Then he turned around and left, nothing more than that.

As for a burial according to custom, I don't know whether

the junta brought those boys home, or moved them to a proper grave elsewhere on the island.

I think of that sometimes. Are all those Argentinean soldiers still piled down in the crevasse where we tossed them that afternoon?

Perhaps it's a question I'll never quite know the answer to.

When the sun went down that day, we watched 2 Para launch their vicious attack across the way on Tumbledown. It was a spectacular sight.

Combat looked hard from where we sat. The tracer fire raced across the hillside. White phosphorous exploded, lighting the dark sky throughout the night.

I remember sitting back with Gaz. We were in our comfortable bivouac, cup of tea in hand. We kept saying how lucky we were to be so far from all of that shite.

Also that night, the Battle of Wireless Ridge was waged.

By the following morning, British military forces had taken each of the seven hills in a five-mile arc around Port Stanley. We crawled out of our tents and all that seemed to remain ahead in our sights was taking back the main city.

Anticipation was high. Chatter became more frequent on the radio; the rumor that Stanley had already fallen to the British was difficult to ignore.

Keeping focus became more difficult. I kept reminding myself that the war was still on. The Argentineans had not surrendered yet.

On the afternoon of June 14th, our section drew patrol. We were ordered down the slope of Mount Harriet.

This patrol was no different than our usual routine. A couple of sections took their combat detail and descended in an arrowhead formation into the valley below. We were well aware of what all the fighting the previous night meant. The surrounding hills were ours and the Argentineans were on the run, routed from their positions.

Our patrol started off as expected. Halfway down, though, we encountered a rag tag group of Argentinean soldiers. There must have been twenty, scurrying out from the rocks and grass. It was like they were happy to see us.

Everyone froze in their tracks.

I was ready for a skirmish. My finger went to the trigger, prepared to fire. Before we had a chance to think the encounter through, their hands shot up in the air.

The soldiers were surrendering. Someone went down to fetch them. My trigger finger eased some, but I remained alert.

As those soldiers came back up the hill toward us in a single file line, my GPMG stayed trained on them. I was ready to fire in the instance that one of those bastards made a stupid move. No one did though. I was relieved. It is a bizarre comfort when your enemy makes a wise choice and allows you to spare their life.

I never saw the whites of their eyes, but I could tell they were bloody scared. Those soldiers had witnessed the same combat that we had on Mount Tumbledown; maybe they had taken part, engaged in vicious, hard-scrabbled fighting.

While we were emboldened by the spectacle, the fight had scared them off.

Soon after returning from patrol, the movement orders came down once again. Our section was among the next to move toward Stanley.

The rumors of Argentinean surrender were rampant by this point. Still, we were ordered onto the coast road in firing positions. Nothing would be left to chance.

Fears that we would be on this God forsaken rock until November were suddenly abated. They were replaced by the sense that we had already won the war.

I am not the kind of person who gives into hearsay. As I packed my fighting order, I had not given over to that feeling of victory.

I remember being optimistic. I remember being filled with hope that we might get some decent rest sooner than we'd feared. But did I think the war was over? All I knew is what I heard from Lou.

Move out, let's go.

I threw my Bergen over my shoulder. I slung my GPMG over the other and prepared for the yomp down off that mountain, on the road to Stanley.

We were five miles out. It was getting near dusk.

I remember the coast road. It opened up wide before us. There were barren stretches of familiar grassland as far as the eye could see.

The road to victory is a hard one for a soldier to forget.

There is a famous picture from that day. It is of a Royal Marine, yomping toward Stanley with a Union Jack splayed across his pack.

I don't remember seeing anyone toting flags around. Even if it was staged, the shot made for a bloody good photo op.

A Royal British Marine, marching into town, ready to take Government House.

PART IV: Aftermath

Chapter 14
The Surrender

Formal surrender came on the evening of June 14th, 1982. That was a Monday; the day of the week was a fact that meant very little to any of the Marines who took the yomp down off of Mount Harriet. What mattered to us was where we were going. And more than that, what would greet us when we finally got there.

The unraveling of the Falkland Island War began as so many do, with a formal cease-fire between the combatants. Few, if any, of the lads who marched down the road toward Stanley knew that was the case though. Of course, there was a healthy amount of conjecture running about, but even at the brink of surrender, we remained mushrooms.

I can remember feeling assured that the major battles were over and done. The Argentineans had been all but driven out of their positions around the main town. It seemed to us that taking Stanley back was all that remained for us to accomplish. And to everyone in our section, we were anxious for that opportunity.

As dawn broke, I could see the lines of enemy soldiers retreating toward Stanley. They evidently had had enough. A few sections had already moved off of Tumbledown by the time we hit the road that morning. They were already well on their way. Our section took up positions behind them, spaced five meters apart. In single file, our weapons remained drawn, no one on either side.

We were positioned as though a fight was what we were in for.

Many images from that morning remain vivid to me. Everyone was quiet. A few paces ahead of me, Gaz crept, his eyes shooting back and forth between road sides. A few kilometers down that road, we passed the barracks at Moody Brook. Once a focal point of our conflict, on that morning it resembled a forgotten ruin. There was a lonesome air hanging about the abandoned buildings, bomb-cratered and still smoking. Only ten weeks earlier, those buildings were destined to be my home for a year.

There was a wide-open field all around the road. As we had seen many times before, the tussock grass was littered with kits, Argentinean weapons and equipment, abandoned in the haste to surrender. There were bodies, although only a few.

As we approached the outskirts of Stanley, Lou ordered our section off the road. We ducked into a Nissen hut, a military structure common from World War II. We filled into the fabricated steel walls, grateful to be out of the wind. Although there was a Red Cross symbol painted on the hut's domed top, plainly visible from the air, the walls and ceiling were riddled with bullet holes, allowing tiny shafts of light to criss-cross the domed shape, shooting down onto the dirt floor.

I still have a picture from inside of that Nissen hut. I don't recall the picture being taken, or what time of day, but there is an other-worldly quality to the air.

We would end up holing up in the Nissen hut for most of the early part of that day. Finally offered the chance to get some rest, most of the lads bagged out. There were no heaters; the only heat came from the Hexi blocks, where lads prepared their cups of tea and what passed for meals.

Our mood was relief. We were coming to the end. In spite of the bullet holes, a constant reminder of the conflict around us, we were out of the rain and wind. We huddled together close in that shed. We cracked jokes, played games, and told stories; we did whatever we could to keep those spirits up.

As for my feet, they were still fucked. I was beyond complaining about it though. I swapped the same two pairs of Marine commando Arctic socks back and forth, pulling the very wet pair off in favor of not so wet. The pain was intense; all I could hope was that the end was indeed as near as it felt. We felt the war was coming to a close, but there was still the lingering question on everybody's mind as to how long we would be on this awful rock. A soldier's life, if nothing, is riddled with worry.

There wasn't much action to serve as distraction to that slow stretch of time. There were little spots of gunfire peppered in the surrounding hills, some explosions; for hours on end, only gusts of wind punctuated the eerie silence. At one point, I remember a half ton bomb going off somewhere in the nearby hills. Distance is difficult to arrive at; those big bastards make a whole lot of noise. The detonation shook my insides something fierce, but once the shockwave dissipated, we settled back down.

A little chatter went out over the radio. Word went over the wire from HQ that Jim McKay's section had turned up missing; there was a search on to locate them.

If the war was over, we had not been told yet. The day

dragged on. I remember bagging out next to Gaz and getting some sleep. I remember thinking, I sure as hell hope those other lads don't seize all the glory. After all, we were the poor bastards whose surrender had made the evening news.

I don't know the exact time the call came, but it must have been a little after midday. All of the lads from NP8901 were being called into Stanley.

We took to the road, not knowing why we had been requested. We were set in a single file line again, spaced five meters apart. Nothing in the town seemed familiar from a couple of months ago. I don't know if any of the details would have stood out to me.

The sky was dark. It felt like nighttime. All of the houses and streetlights were out. Businesses were boarded up. As we advanced from the outskirts, into the main part of town, you could hardly tell we were in a populated place, let alone a war zone. Stanley felt to me then like a ghost town.

As we approached the grounds surrounding Government House, I saw there were lights on, and then I caught sight of a few people. There were soldiers, British soldiers. By now, night had fallen. It was 20:00. Approaching friendly faces, I picked up my pace.

It was over that short stretch, following Gaz up the hedge-lined path toward those grand front doors that the moment grabbed hold of me: there was something curious afoot here.

I had an unshakably eerie feeling returning to that scene; I think a few of the other lads would have agreed. Our shame out front of the stately building had been burned into my memory, and this was my clearest reminder. Surely, I was not alone in wanting to end up back here so badly that, at times, the feeling was palpable. Now that I was here, though, unsure of our charge, I was overcome with anxiety.

One by one, we were ushered into the main lobby. Once we were in position at the bottom of the main staircase, we were ordered to wait.

Here we go again, I thought. Hurry up and wait.

I leaned against the wall. We were like a collection of toy soldiers, barely able to stand upright from fatigue. I was exhausted and surely rank. Every piece of clothing that was draped across my body was in tatters and covered in a layer of muck and bog filth from forty awful days out in the field. We must have been quite the sight.

After waiting what felt like hours, we heard the front doors open and shut. Someone shouted out, "Attention."

Before we could snap though, Major Jeremy Moore strutted into the lobby. He was followed by his attaché. Their heads were held high. And they expected the same.

Immediately, Moore shot a glare in my direction. I remember through the severity of his look that his handsome appearance stood out like a sore thumb. For the life of me, I could not recall the last time I saw someone clean-shaven and presentable.

I saluted the Major and his men. For that half-assed effort, I got a seething glare. They looked at me like I was nothing more than a common road apple. The lad beside me got much worse though. He remained slouched like a limp rag against the wall for maybe a second longer, and for that, he took a harsh bollicking. Moore must have seen his delay as lazy insolence.

Then, as quick as the party entered the lobby, they disappeared in an officious line up the main staircase. They ended up spending quite a long time on the second floor; there were no clocks nearby, but it felt like forever. We heard nary a peep, but were fully aware that we were responsible for their wellbeing. For the duration of their conference, I stood ramrod straight. My suddenly hawkish eyes were forward.

About an hour later, we heard doors open and close. Moore and his attaché walked down the hall and descended the stairs. By then, we got a look at their faces.

Then, finally, we got word of what everyone was gathered there to do. The Argentinean forces had signed surrender documents.

Bloody hell, I thought. Really?

The history books record their signatures at one minute short of 2100 hours. Whatever, I was not aware of the time as reality sunk in. The Falkland Island War was over.

I never saw General Mario Menendez in Government House that night. He must have been there, though, as his signature appears on those surrender documents.

The last lines of Argentinean defense around Stanley had been broken down. During the previous day's fighting, one of their company commanders got lost, an inexplicable occurrence. As a result, all of his junior commanders became despondent, uncertain what to do next. The chain of command was broken.

Long after the war was over, Santiago Carrizo, a private serving in their third Regiment, would describe how Argentinean troops had been positioned in houses around Stanley. Their orders were to shoot any enemies on sight;

none of them did though. They threw up their hands instead. They were done with fighting.

Sounds like a bloody lot of chaos. No wonder they threw up their hands.

The Argentinean military works with a strictly defined code for surrender. That code states that unless more than half the men were casualties, or seventy-five percent of the ammo had been spent, a surrender would be deemed illegal; none of those conditions had been met during the Falkland conflict. That hardly seemed to matter at all to Menendez. His troops had simply given up, no longer willing or able to resist. Better for them, and a hell of a lot better for us.

A lot of official mumbo jumbo got thrown into those documents, terminology in place in order to make the surrender legal. None of the lads I spoke to gave one shite about what went into those negotiations, outside of the end result. Whatever gets you through the night. It was over.

With surrender papers signed, reality began to sink in. Moore and the rest of the military hierarchy departed Government House, meaning we were released from our duty. There was nothing to watch over anymore.

Soon, we discovered that there were others in the house, rollicking about. We could hear their footsteps and shouts. An all-out party had begun.

We moved out to the dining hall, where we met up with the other victorious lads. By now, word had spread and every-one was celebrating. To this very day, I don't remember what we ate, but we feasted on real food, not the packaged crap from our ration box, heated in a shell scrape with a Hexi block. No more military issue tea or coffee either. I remember the wine clearly. The whole thing was like the scene from the Last Supper, only instead of apostles, it was a bunch of dirty-faced lads talking shite.

Government House was where the Argentinean brass had set up their command. We helped ourselves to shelves lined with exotic South American wines and brandy. We drank whatever we could find and hardly spared a drop. To us, there was no tomorrow, and our lusty cheers went up, wine spilled without care for the linens.

"Fuck all" was the sentiment. "We just won a bloody war!"

Surrounded by a lot of drunk, filthy blokes, I had the time of my life.

I have been to a lot of parties in my time and many of them are forgettable, to be entirely truthful.

That one though, the night of June 14th, I'll never forget.

We yomped back and spent that night back in the Nissen hut. The next morning, we turned around and returned to Stanley, where we began the task of cleaning up.

Even a small war leaves a mess in its wake. Nearly twelve thousand Argentinean soldiers had been taken prisoner over the short course of the war. Those men had to be dealt with in a proper, humane fashion, according to convention. On top of what turned out to be a fair-sized human mess, we were also tasked with solving the enormous problem of unexploded munitions. We found abandoned stores of rocket shells, napalm canisters, and a slew of anti-aircraft missiles strewn around all over the city streets.

What also became clear, as our forces gradually reclaimed the Falklands, was the extent to which the Argentinean military had mined the territory surrounding Stanley. There were a great number of mines, a problem only compounded by their method and record keeping. Normally following a miner's logbook can make the task of deactivating active mines simple, but their records were an absolute joke. They were incomplete and in many places, the mine locations were logged incorrectly. Perhaps out of desperation, the Argentineans had not relied on professional miners to lay their minefields. Any of their units, from basic infantry to artillery, were allowed to lay mines. As a result, the markers were missing, or had shifted off in deep sand. Cleaning that up would be dangerous, to say the least. I felt lucky that wasn't our charge.

Had the bastards stopped at simply laying shoddy landmines, it would have been enough. There was more though. In the later stages of the conflict, as defeat became imminent, they booby-trapped civilian houses where they had been holed up. They linked explosives to anything they could find, with a special fondness for bombing attractive family heirlooms like binoculars and knick-knacks that, to a returning Islander, would seem safely undisturbed. Pick up that antique clock and, boom.

Their vindictiveness saw no limits, and the desperation of their situation only became clearer as those sorting days pressed on. Argentinean soldiers opened up taps in the houses and turned on fire hydrants, taxing the island's already fragile water supply. They burned down the Globe Store in town, thinking their commanders were cooped up safely in there. Mutiny wasn't just a rumor; it was a stark reality.

We heard the officers had kept their side arms ready. Without them, they would not have survived long enough to surrender.

The landscape was chaos.

I had a bloody hangover from the previous night's bout of drinking. By then, however, it was my feet that were fucked beyond repair.

As a result, I was relegated to house duty. While the other lads in my section set about escorting prisoners off of the island, or cleaning up the streets, I stuck around Government House. Some of the guys gave me shit for begging off, Gaz in particular. Did I care? Not really. I had done everything in my power to stay on my feet throughout those last grueling forty days; and by then, I didn't mind keeping off of them.

Alone in Government House, I got bored—such luxury. At last I was warm and dry, and that was all I bloody cared about. Left to my own devices, I wandered around the large, stately house, taking in details of the hallways and bedrooms. The place felt different than it had my first time, probably because I wasn't racing up the staircase with a GPMG on my shoulder, getting a bollicking for breaking precious window glass.

Many of the lads had taken souvenirs from Government House the night before. Proffing was rampant. The Argentineans had surrendered quite hastily. The house had served as their command center, so they ended up leaving a great deal of their stuff around. I watched as guys walked out with fine China and spoons, helping themselves to any of the military paraphernalia strewn about. I remember one Marine taking an ancient pair of dueling pistols, centuries old antiques that had once belonged to some General. Now they were going home, smuggled like smut in some bloke's duffel bag. As of yet, I hadn't taken anything.

It must have been early afternoon when I wandered into one of the upstairs bedrooms. As far as I could tell, there was no one around, so I felt comfortable nosing around in a few of the personal affects scattered about.

In a bedside table, I found a photo album. Bored stiff, I started leafing through the pages when I discovered a set of pictures of General Mario Menendez of the Argentine Army, posed with President Armando Galltieri, all of the photos taken on the Falkland Islands. No one knew that Galltieri had been here; here was the proof of that.

Holy shit, I thought. This is one of a kind. I have got to take this back.

The room suddenly took on a new meaning. This was the bedroom where General Menendez had slept only a few nights before. Quickly, I tucked the photo album under my arm and began to search for whatever keepsakes I could find.

On the floor beneath the bed, I dragged out a pair of military boots. The leather felt new, smelled of polish. They were fine, not the battered black dogs that we wore. They were high quality leather that shined so brightly you could see your reflection.

I tried them on; they fit my feet perfectly.

What the hell, I thought. May as well take these too. Quite happy with my spoils, I scurried off to secure these treasures in with the rest of my kit.

Two and a half months can go by in the blink of an eye; for me, it went quicker.

On the morning of April 2nd, 1982, I had been forced face down onto the cold courtyard stone outside the front steps of Government House. My weapon had been seized.

My hands were up. A bunch of Argentinean commandos, mugging for the camera, surrounded my prone form. That was a dubious moment, not just in my life, but in the proud course of British history as well.

All of the lads in that picture had been seething ever since, and it was on June 17th that we finally got the chance to restore order.

The moment started off in an ordinary fashion. A Marine is never told to pause and savor the moment; he must simply follow orders. Lou ordered our section down out of the house, where we were to gather in the courtyard. Just like always, we followed, trudging back out into the bracing cold, where a Union Jack awaited us.

It was then that I recognized what would come next.

Out of the small crowd of waiting Marines and personnel, the lads of NP8901 were called out to the front. Moments from glory, we gathered at the base of the flagpole. Then everything ground to an awkward halt. Presumably, we were all waiting on a photographer to get his shit together.

There was no big band on the scene. No one cued up a crackling old recording of "God Save the Queen" to stir our hearts. Nobody stood on ceremony, nor did anyone of the Generals utter a patriotic word of cheer to mark the historic moment.

We attached the flag to its lanyard and raised it high into the sky. Then we stood back and watched it rippling in the wind.

For the life of me, I cannot recall seeing that photographer snapping pictures in our midst; not that I was looking for him though. I was, as I had been up until then, living the moment without a shred of pretense.

All the books about the Falkland Island War show that moment: a scrum of salty, bog-splattered Marines clamoring to get their filthy hands on the dangling lanyard.

I do clearly recall, though, that the moment felt pretty damn good. NP8901 had all come full circle. Look it up. Take a look at the picture. You can see my mug right there. Those are my hands and eyes reaching skyward.

The moment was fleeting. What exists in memory for a lifetime only lasted a few seconds before it was over.

Once the Union Jack was up in that stiff wind over Government House, signaling a return to British reign, we were ordered back to our chores.

Over and done, all without a spare moment to take it in.

Chapter 15
The Long Ride Home

How much longer are we going to stick around on this bloody rock?

This was the question that lingered on everyone's mind as the long days unfurled after the Argentinean surrender.

We lived in the Nissen hut. We were back to eating rations again. There would be no more feasts on the Government House linens. Our weapons remained loaded and ready for combat. Winter bit down hard around us. The weather only got worse.

We had a sense that NP8901 had been given special treatment. A few of the guys had speculated that our role in the fight had been, at least in part, PR. Once that flag went back up over Government House though, we were treated like any grunt Marines. Nothing special, no one making certain we were pushed to the front of the line.

Once the photo op had been executed, we were just like everybody else. I am certain that the newspapers at home ate all that patriotic shite up. Here they were, the lads who had surrendered, back to raise the bloody Union Jack.

We were back in the day-to-day slog. We were running regular operations, collecting rations. There was live ammo in all of our weapons. The fear increased that we would be stuck here for an interminable time; time only aggravated that.

As it turns out though, we were turned back home within a few short days.

I remember Lou stalking into the Nissen hut one afternoon. With a look that teetered on the brink of a smile, he examined the lot of us.

What are you mugging for? We all thought, waiting on his word. I'm sure every one of us expected him to announce another crap chore; clean up this, or clean up that.

Instead he said, time to go. Pack up your kit lads, we are leaving in an hour.

I don't quite recall if a cheer went up, but one thing is for certain. There was a new spring in our step as we got our stuff together. We were going home.

As it turns out, those long days on the Falklands was simply waiting on our ride to arrive. After a short trip transporting a stock of prisoners across the sea to port in Argentina, the SS Canberra returned to the waters off the Falkland Islands.

As we all stepped onto the troop transport, similar to the one that we had made landfall in at San Carlos water months ago, we saw her sitting on the water.

What a sight for sore eyes. Here we go again, I thought. Heading back home the same way we came in.

The two-week trip home was nothing like the ride we had taken to the Falklands. A sense of relief prevailed in our section, in place of trepidation. Rather than stash the lot of us in servant's quarters below the water line, we had better rooms up on sea deck. We still had to share a room with another Marine, but we had baths and showers.

It was late in June; for the first time since early April, I got to take a proper bath. Watching all that bog wash down the drain was surreal.

We had a bathtub that was loaded up with ice. The blokes that served us our meals kept that generously stocked with cans of beer.

Any time that we wanted to, we could dip into that tub for a cold lager, or an ale. Boy did we ever indulge. We weren't too far into our northward course before I had a case of frostbite from dipping my paw in there for a beer. Even then, nothing was going to slow us down from drinking.

None of us had seen a woman in months, let alone touched one. We talked about it quite a lot and daydreamed even more. That's all we had to go on though—a few words and our fantasies, not a lot for a young man.

Back then, combat forces weren't integrated like they are today. Nowadays, a lad in my boots would at least have a chance to flirt with a female soldier in the field.

Gaz had put it bloody perfectly up there on Wall Mountain. He had spent more nights by my side in the Falklands than he ever had with his girlfriend. It had been a long time since that night I'd gone to see the UK Subs perform back home, and my send-off present. We were all pretty randy by now; I know I was. And similar to the constant flow of beer in the tub, someone in the British military knew how to take care of us.

A couple of the newspapers back home had put out regular advertisements, seeking female pen pals for lonesome soldiers fighting down in the Falkland Islands. The request was phrased innocently enough, I suppose. We were all out there fighting and putting our lives on the line for their country and the military wanted letters from any ladies willing to share a few kind, encouraging words to a hopeful Marine.

Bloody brilliant, I thought. They're setting us up for a welcome home.

None of us knew that this kind of thing was coming for us when we stepped on board the Canberra, but there they were, massive mail sacks, filled with hand written letters waiting for us to dive in. It was unreal. Between these and all that beer, I felt like a little boy given free rein in a sweet shop. Every envelope that we tore open had a letter and a cutesy little snapshot of a single girl, eager to help spread cheer.

That wasn't all we were hoping would spread for us though.

We devoured those letters like starved wolves. Even the married guys and those with girlfriends got in on the act. We had a hell of a lot of fun sitting around in our rooms, reading letters out loud and making sport in how we ranked their pictures. Thinking back, we came across as quite cruel. We set up a gronk (total loser) board where we posted pictures of the girls we thought were ugly, making jokes and ridicule. The pretty girls got gobbled up pretty quick. They were treated like commodities, and a few of the lads got quite territorial with sorting out who was going to score each one.

If I had been randy before, this endeavor only served to peak my interest further. All of those willing ladies, I felt like an animal.

Before the Canberra even set sail, I was busy writing letters, setting up meetings for the day we returned. The way I saw it, there was no use leaving anything to chance. I never had much reason to write home before; perhaps I was just missing the type of incentive that was a lovely girl. A great deal of my time on board the Canberra was spent responding to letters. I think I wrote more letters home to those pen pals than I did during the rest of my service combined. Two or three times throughout that trip, mail drops were made, with bulging sacks of letters headed back to Pool in Dorset county.

I'm sure a few of those were addressed to wives and mothers and sons, from Marines who were eager to see loved ones again.

I did my best though to keep those sacks stuffed with pen pal letters. After two months in the Falkland muck and bog alongside Gaz, I was fixing for a woman's company.

We drank a bloody lot on board the Canberra. We sent out our pen pal letters whenever we had a chance. Regardless of diversions though, there was still work to do.

We trained hard daily. We ran and yomped about on the deck. There was no longer any live ammunition in our weapons, but we still kept in tiptop shape. There was more than exercise as well. It seemed like every day there were lectures and readings to take in, and de-briefings with command to look forward to. The motto for the Royal Marines on that ride may well have been, 'work hard and play even harder'.

I was still driven to stay fit. One of my objectives for deployment to the Falkland Islands was to get in the best shape of my life, and I saw no reason to slow that down. Training has always been something I could drill down and stay focused with.

Although we were on our way home, that did not necessarily mean any of us had been made aware of where we were headed next. As far as the rumor mill was concerned, we could be going anywhere; it seemed as though there was another possibility thrown about with each passing day. The only subject on board the Canberra that provoked more conversation than pen pals and the gronk board was where we were headed.

A few days after the Argentinean forces surrendered on the Falkland Islands, June 20th, British forces retook nearby South Sandwich Island. There was a base there, the Corbeta Uruguay, which had been disputed since 1976 through diplomatic channels. With Argentinean influence in the South Atlantic battered, the Southern Thule Garrison was taken back with ease. We knew that we would not be heading there any time soon.

Tensions in the Middle East had reached a fevered pitch. On June 6th, after repeated skirmishes with the Palestine Liberation Organization, the PLO, Israeli forces invaded southern Lebanon. The invasion sparked the Lebanon War. Rumors spread like wildfire that we would be re-routed to Israel to help the Israelis fight their war. British forces had backed the Israelis in territorial conflicts before; it seemed feasible that we would come to their aid now as well.

Israel in June sounded warm, almost inviting, compared to the God forsaken wind and rain of the Falkland Islands. No one wanted any part of that fight though. Those rumors began to rage out of control, and there was no impulse to quell them.

The cycle of life on board Canberra was set. Train hard. Drink harder. Plot your dream date for the day you get home, if you got there. Go to bed each night and pray in hopes that you do.

Surrender meant the end of the war between the British and Argentinean armies. June 14th did not, however, mean an end to all the conflicts.

We were done with bullets and bombs, but there was still the matter of a few bloodied lips to square a few old scores. The term "brothers in arms" does not necessarily mean that everyone gets along all hunky dory. A pair of brothers, after all, will fight like no other. On board the Canberra, one of those scores that needed settling was the grudge that Danny was holding onto. He had to get his revenge, and on that ride back home was the perfect time to get it.

I remember the Corporal's name that had shunned him on Wall Mountain but have chosen to leave it out.

Military justice is simple; it works in one of two clear ways. There is nary a gray area between these two poles. A soldier can seek his justice in a military court. Or he can take it by his own bare hands. Those are the two ways right there—plead for justice or fight for revenge.

The way Danny saw it, his situation was quite clear. There was not a military court in all of England that would prosecute Corporal Bryant for denying him shelter. What happened up on Wall Mountain wasn't that kind of offense; there wasn't treason or a break with protocol. The offense was man to man, right from wrong between brothers. Danny would have to steer the other way toward revenge, and for that he would need to recruit his mates instead. And as it turns out, they were more than happy to help him mete out a rough dose of justice.

As I recall, Danny hardly had to ask them twice.

We were pissing up (drinking) in my bedroom, just like we did every night. There were at least six or seven lads piled up on the bunk beds, or sitting cross-legged on the floor. We had been hammering beers and talking shite about girls all night long. What we were going to do to so-and-so when we got home. Maybe we had been sorting out the possibility of getting shuffled onto some war in the Middle East, I don't know, but we must have been a hundred pints of ale into the night before someone asked a question.

"What are we going to do about him?"

Nobody needed to clarify any further. Everyone knew which person "him" was referring to. Everyone knew as well what situation we were talking about.

At the drop of a hat, Butch was keen. The way he answered the call immediately, I swear he had been preparing for that very moment ever since Danny came shivering near death into our camp.

"Let's kill him," Butch said, a gleam of seriousness racing through his eyes. "Just let me get my boots on first, aright?"

I swear, that man was serious. And as a few others agreed, I knew they were too. Revenge had been agreed on, and it would be the roughest possible.

His room just happened to be next to mine. We hadn't heard a peep all night from over there; he was probably sleeping quietly as the conspirators gathered around my door. I opted to stay behind, but the rest of the lads got busy masking their faces, armed up with weapons and slipped out, as quiet as ghosts.

For a moment, everything was silent. I took a deep, anticipatory breath.

Then I remember hearing the next chamber door over knock down, followed by a stream of bodies rushing in. They acted like Commandos, moving efficiently, with the kind of stealth few people live to describe. I remember the sound of a thunder flash going off in that room like a grenade, and the helpless wails as they battered him good. By the sound of things, they got a pretty thorough beating in on him. When things got quiet again, they moved out. Then moments later, one by one, everyone came back into my room and pulled off their masks.

By the satisfied looks on their faces, justice had been doled out. Danny was beaming from ear to ear. His moment of revenge was actualized.

A few more beers were cracked, cold cans cradled in bruised hands. I don't quite recall, but we all probably started talking girls again.

"What are you going to do, John?"

"Oh," I would say. "Can't wait to get my hands up inside her skirt."

Military justice is quick. It deploys fast and it moves on even faster still.

Danny got revenge in what we came to refer to as a kangaroo court. This route was a hell of a lot more immediate and satisfying than the bureaucratic route.

By the break of morning, he could hold his head high again.

Those guys beat him within an inch of his life that night. With him pinned helplessly down to his bed, unable to resist the onslaught of fists and batons, maybe only the fatigue of so many vicious blows at once saved his life. To my eyes, it did not seem as though discretion played a part. As they left the room and he rolled over on his side, spitting blood and teeth, he had to know how he got here.

He had to know it was Danny's call to go commando on him.

Even now, as I think back on it, I cannot quite say why I didn't join in the beating. Down in my gut though, I knew to stay back. Perhaps it was an underlying feeling that I had already done my part on Danny's behalf by simply letting him into my tent. Perhaps it was something even more than that, revulsion from that kind of behavior.

Whatever it was, I don't care to scour for further meaning. Any way we could look at it, justice had been served and the slate was clean.

Had this fellow chosen to get up off the deck to report what had happened, no one would listen to him. He was hardly recognizable the next morning, a bruised and bloody mess; odds are someone asked what happened. And if I had to venture a guess to his reply, he would have said something like he had slipped in the shower.

Whether or not they believed him, that's bloody likely what he would have said.

Military justice is a curious sort of institution. A soldier cannot just beat another soldier senseless for no reason at all, especially a ranking officer. If there is good reason though, then the idea of justice shifts some. Chris had to know that he had rightfully earned that beating. He probably dreaded something like this was coming for him beginning the night after he had spurned a freezing brother. Maybe as he rolled over and tried to put his face back together, he was relieved to have it over and done with.

No more waiting. No more peeking around corners to see who might be lurking. Having your beating done seems like it might be quite a relief.

Even if he had chosen to go up the chain of command with his pair of black eyes and broken nose, Butch and Danny and the rest were no fools. They had gone into that room like military men, trained to act swiftly and efficiently. There is no justice to be gotten with masked men; the whole ship would have fit the attacker's description. Who was he going to possibly point to as his assailants? They had crept up on him at night, careful to wear masks. And no one in that room had said a bloody word, except Chris, whining and begging all pathetic like for help. If Lou had gathered us all up on deck, asking who had done such a thing, no one was going to raise a hand to volunteer.

There is a sweet efficiency in military justice; a bittersweet quality that civilians simply cannot quite understand.

The next day we were all called out to the swimming pool. Moans and groans. Another picture. Another photo op for the victorious army.

As tedious as it seemed, I thought, best enjoy the regalia now.

Photos are strange to look back on. I have meditated on that fact enough already. Each picture tells a story to anyone looking at it, but unless you're in the snapshot, the tale is impressionistic, or otherwise clipped, incomplete.

We are all in a celebratory mood in that picture. Everyone is wearing training shorts and looking a tad ragged, the kind of unkempt look from letting your hair down. We're posing like we're on holiday, a bunch of lads taking a week-long cruise.

This guy is there in that picture. For me, it's easy to pick him out. He's the one with black eyes, his face swollen up like a sweet melon.

He's doing his best to smile, but he cannot. He looks utterly miserable kneeling there, and deservedly so. The selfish bastard almost cost one of NP8901 his life.

I still have that picture.

Moments of arrival and departure burn onto our memories. The day we arrived home to England is one I will never forget, so long as I draw breath.

Every one of us had the day circled. We had to know that it was coming because we all had been writing our pen pals, telling them when we would be able to meet up. Some lads counted down the days till that moment; I had it down to a matter of hours.

We saw land appear on the horizon. As we hurried about in preparation for our arrival back in port, command ordered us that we were not to carry any weapons off of the boat. If we had any contraband weapons, customs would seize them. Any of the lads who had been cribbing knives and pistols, something proffed during the war, promptly dropped them somewhere safe, where they could come back later for them.

I had not expected anyone to greet me there in South Hampton. That lonesome truth was simply part of being a single man. There were Gaz and Danny and me, and we boasted about being the Lone Rangers, bachelor soldiers without anyone to speak of.

Whether it was the excitement of arrival or pent up anxiety, I am not sure; but that morning I got hammered. I was not going to let all the free beer I could drink go without a fight and as the ship pulled into port, I was downing cans one after another.

It was a lovely summer day in South Dorsett. An impressive crowd started gathering there along the docks to greet the Canberra early that morning. The cheers were loud.

Happy mothers and children waved frantically from the docks, leaning out hopeful for a first look at their returning loved ones. We could see the colorful banners streaming in the breeze from a few kilometers out. It was breathtaking. We got our deserved dose of all the glittering pomp and circumstance afforded to returning victors.

As I walked down the plank, waving to no one in particular, Mom stepped out of the crowd. I do not know how she knew, maybe the news, but she boxed my ears sternly and gave me the kind of run around you expect when you're a bad six year old.

"Eight in the morning," she said, "and you're already pissed?"

I harrumphed, probably saying something under my breath to appease her. Mom was the last person I had expected to see, except maybe Dad. Either way, as I soaked up that glorious moment, it was her admonishing voice that rang in my head.

As the crowd noise slowly dimmed in the distance, we were all crowded into a long line of waiting coaches. One by one, we boarded until there were fifty or sixty Marines cramped in each bus, where we settled down for the long drive back to base.

The South Dorsett streets were lined with people. It seemed that around every turn, we encountered another adoring crowd, strangers leaning in toward the streaming buses to wave and blow kisses at us. The celebratory feeling was surreal; maybe too much all at once. The victory that was once ours, now belonged to everyone else.

That entire hour and a half drive felt like a dream.

Once we were back at base in Pool, we ditched our kit and

got into civilian clothes. That felt quite good, I recall. The last layer of Falkland misery stripped away. Now that we had arrived, we were free to do as we pleased. A few of the lads with families at home went back and spent that first night there, and bloody good for them.

I had no such encumbrances though.

I had set up dates that night with a few of the choice pen pals I had selected. As far as plans go, mine was quite simple. Once in my civilian clothes, I would saunter down to the Jolly Miller bar in Pool and cozy up with whichever one I pleased.

So much detail escapes me, but I do remember that she was quite pretty. She had a cute figure and wore glasses. I remember that I had liked those from her pictures.

We didn't bother talking for very long at the bar, but from our brief conversation, I gathered that she worked as a nurse. She had an apartment in one of the buildings shared with the rest of the hospital staff. All that sounded good enough to me. For all I cared in that moment, she could have lived under the bloody bridge.

I cannot remember her name now. What has burned clear though, is that we spent my first night back in England together at her apartment. There was not much talking done there either, to tell the truth. That girl wasn't interested in hearing about the Falkland Islands. She wanted to show me gratitude, and boy did she ever show it. That was one hell of a night.

I will never know if what she was doing amounted to a pity shag; maybe there were other dates lined up for her. Frankly, I didn't much care then, and I don't care now. After all of those cold nights sacked out in the rain, in

Nissen huts and in shell scrapes next to Gaz, this was what I had dreamt of all along.

A woman's warmth was what kept me warm. At last, I had it again.

I remember waking up early that next morning. Old Marine habits can be tough to shake off. Rain was pounding on the window. Wind rattled the glass.

I sighed deeply as I rolled off of the bed. She continued sleeping peacefully, her back turned to me as if to say, go ahead, leave if you have to.

Mission accomplished, I thought.

Then I quietly pulled on my clothes. I didn't wake her up to say thank you for the evening, or goodbye. After that morning, I never saw that girl again, fine by me. Even though I had awoken, even though I had to report back to base, I was still living in a dream.

Every Marine who served in the Falklands shared a similar fear. We all were pained with the thought that we would be sent back. Considering the circumstance, this fear was not an unfounded one; most of us were, after all, on a year's deployment there, and out of that, only six months had passed by. We very well could have ended up on that wind swept rock for the remaining six months, serving out our sentence as a garrison.

As it turns out though, I would never go back to the Falkland Islands.

When I returned to base that morning, I learned that NP8901 had been dissolved. As a result, we were ordered to put our names in for a new assignment.

All right, I thought, *we've been spared that awful fate.*

The Royal Marines have a recruitment company, R-Company, as it is commonly referred to. Marines serving in that company travel out to all the little country towns, wearing polished boots and their dress uniforms. They shake hands and tell every one of those adoring people what it's like to serve in the RMC; they're a well-armed PR firm. Danny, Gaz and I had heard that the commanders in R-company had enough hard case WWII vets; they wanted to bring in a few young lads who had served in the Falklands, making our bright smiling faces seem like the perfect candidates. R-Company is quite competitive though; only thirty or so lads serve there at a time.

Whatever, I thought. I'll cast my lot there. I deserved a cushy order and I wanted to stay in Pool, where the summers are like heaven.

Who was I kidding? I wanted to be where the girls were. They would flock in droves to a lad in uniform with a heroic story. If I was going to stay in Pool, it would be one of two ways, either serving in R-Company or the SBS, Speed Boat Service. I put in for the former.

After putting in for our new orders, we were all given six weeks home leave. With my time off, I went back home and stayed with Dad. There was nowhere else for me to go.

I got drunk every night over that month and a half. I'm not talking just tipsy, mind you; I got all-out hammered, every single night, until I reported back to base.

I didn't think quite this way back then, but I have been blessed with an uncanny ability to put the unpleasant things aside and live in the now, in the moment.

For me, in those days, drinking so much wasn't reckless, nor was it foolish. That forty-day blind drunk bender was how I cleared my head.

It's how I put aside all the shite I had seen back there in the Falklands.

During that leave, a few of us got together and took a short excursion. We went out to a town called Skegness, a tiny seaside resort spot up along the North Sea coast.

It was still the summer, although getting late in the season. All we wanted was to be where there was warmth and water. We wanted to be where the girls were.

We crowded into a single hotel room. Maybe the front desk people gave us a funny look, so many lads cramped into a single room, but they had no idea where we had been before. That's part of the struggle in coming home, I think; no one really knows what hell you've been through, aside from you and your brother. There are times when that brother by your side is all you've got.

None of us had any grand designs on taking in the sights. Instead, we spent those few days in the bars, drinking hard and fighting. Whenever we got our rage that way, we were back to our old tricks, trapping ladies without a bloody care in the world.

Danny was there. So was Gaz. So were a few of the choice lads from the former NP8901 who were without families and on the lookout for something to do. In those days, these were the only lads who could really understand me.

Those days up in Skegness were good times. We drank quite a lot. Those nights on the beach were the sort that you fondly recall not remembering much about.

Good times end though, just like the bad times do.

Soon, we had to leave Skegness; sooner still it seemed, we were all due to report back to base in Pool. Our leave was coming to a close, such a bloody lot of melancholy.

When I got back to base, I remember looking at the orders board to learn my fate — I had gotten my wish, and so had Gaz. We were going to be a part of R-Company.

Chapter 16
Service & Later Years

For another seven years, I served in the Royal Marines before getting out. For at least half of those years, I carted around that same red, Argentinean sleeping bag I proffed from a tent with me. Even after I was making enough soldier's pay on my own that I could afford to buy my swankier kit, it was still the warmest bag I'd ever slept in. That bag went with me everywhere. Where it went though, I don't recall.

Gaz and I served out our glorious time in R-Company, after which we were forced to move on. The importance of the Falkland Island War ebbed in the national conscience, and suddenly, our experience wasn't quite as relevant anymore.

On that awful rock, Gaz had been my brother, as close as I'd been to anyone. But even close-knit brothers move onto other things eventually. Somewhere along the line, we got other orders and parted. Further on down the line, he got out and so did I.

Something I don't recall is if we tried to keep in touch. Likely, we did not, instead drifting apart, like so many others from that life tend to do. He went his way and I went mine.

I travelled all around the world with the Royal Marines. During those seven years, I touched some of the most remote and beautiful places on planet Earth, only to return home and settle down very close to where I grew up. At some point I thought, here I am, back in the same bloody place that I vowed to escape.

Another of those facts of life taught only through hard experience; that age-old story of the Prodigal Son is, in fact, universal. It is our collective story.

Returning home settled me down; at least it settled me some, enough to get married and see the birth of my son, Charlie. He's my pride. In some ways, he's already a lot like his father, pushing himself in all the sports, always striving to be the best. The apple doesn't fall far from the tree, I'm proud to say.

All my life, I'd had the God-given ability to live in the moment, to only deal with what was out in front of me. Some of that went away when Charlie was born.

Suddenly, I was looking back. I was forced to. I was flooded with reflections on what I had done up till then with my life, with that which brought me here to him. When I started thinking about my service again in this new light, naturally, I reflected on my time in the Falklands.

This story is that reflection.

The Falkland Island War ended thirty-five years ago. That's a lifetime for some men, those unlucky enough to have been buried down there.

Thinking back on those frozen images, I simply cannot recall all of the names. A few stand out, but just as many have escaped me. Even those I do remember, I hardly know the fate of half of those lads.

Eggman killed himself some years after. I don't know whether it had anything to do with taking fire on the hot side of Mount Harriet. But when I heard, that is the first thing that crossed my mind, the scattered, shell-shocked look in his eye as he told us the news.

Combat stress wasn't something you really talked about back then. There was no PTSD to speak of. There was still a stigma, an idea that only the weak expressed vulnerability. This is another way in which war has changed. We fortunately have the notion of opening that line of communication, one that perhaps, in Eggman's case, came along a generation too late.

Had Eggman gotten help, would he still be here today? Who knows? Certainly not an ordinary Marine like me. I hardly like to think of it, to tell the truth.

Gaz is still kicking around. Although he does not live that far away, I hardly have the urge to see him. I don't want to, in fact. We're not estranged, nothing untoward happened between us to cause a rift. Once that chapter closed and we drifted further apart from that awful rock, Gaz became a part of that construct of memory. In the story of my life, his role has been played out already, all described in these pages.

The same can be said for the other lads, like Danny and Butch. If I saw one of them across the bar tomorrow, I would surely come over and say hello. But if they were across a busy street, I would have to think twice. There is something awful in that. Something awful, yet honest.

I remember hearing that the person who'd gotten that beating got a tattoo on his arm, memorializing his time served in NP8901. That news seemed strange, that he would mark himself proudly, considering what he had done and the beating he had taken as a result of it. Had that been me curled up in a bloody, bruised ball on that bed, I would hardly have been able to look myself in the eye, never mind commemorate it. Or perhaps what he'd taken from that beating is more than I can ever understand. Who knows? What men will do to mark their time though, or the stories they tell themselves never ceases to amaze me.

I am certain that some, if not all of my mates from the Falkland Island War, still have their stuff—medals and uniforms and other proffed keepsakes. I do not, however. Years after coming home, most of my stuff ended up stolen from my sister's house. There was a part of me happy to see it go the easy way—all at once.

In that theft, I lost the pictures of Menendez and Galltieri. That album had one-of-a-kind value. Pictures were rare back then, not like today. I like to think of the thief, opening that box up and flipping through those faded snaps. He probably didn't know what he had and tossed them like so much other shite.

Recently, I received my veterans pin in the mail from the Royal Marines. I'm of that age, a relic that gets a medal in the mail for their time.

I was an old sweat; now I'm just old.

You want to know where that medal is? It's in the box it came in, on my shelf. I haven't taken it down and put it on yet. When I look on it now, I doubt that I ever will.

On Remembrance Day each year, I pay my respects. I say a silent work for guys like Eggman, and the host of others I knew who lost their lives in service. In this, I stay connected.

Do I parade around town though? No. When that moment of silence is broken, my life would go on as it had before, when I was younger and very different.

Before Charlie was born, my thoughts rarely drifted back to the Falkland Islands. What happened to me there came out as stories, tossed around the bar with the other old soldiers. That was all they were to me, stories just tossed around for laughs.

There was only once I can recall when I had "a moment." I was traveling through Argentina with my girlfriend at the time. We were in Buenos Aires when we staggered across the Argentinean memorial to the fallen soldiers of Guerra de las Malvinas.

I needed to catch my breath. Although I made the obvious connection being in Argentina, the memorial unexpectedly stirred all those memories back up again. Then it was gone. I choked it back and moved on.

It has been that way for thirty-five years now. Memories of war resurface in glimmers, only to be forced back down. The difference from here on out though, is I have Charlie to answer to. When he gets to a certain age, he will have questions. Kids always do. Who were you, Dad? What did you do? I will need to have answers when that day comes.

The General's boots? I still have those. They are sitting in my father's back yard garden shed, where they have been for as long as I can remember. Stashing them there instead of my sister's house is the only reason I still have them.

The other day, I went to visit my father. I brought him a sachet of tobacco from one of my working trips to the Middle East. On his living room wall is that picture from the Canberra ride home, the guy beaten black and blue, and the lads in trainers—all looking goofy.

Maybe those boots will stay there forever, locked away until the wrecking ball comes to knock the shed down. As my father gets older, I don't feel the need to grab and take them home with me, to use those to break the ice with my son. Those boots do not stand as the legacy of my time in the Falklands.

This story does.

About the Author

John Alden Joined the Royal Marine Commandos at the age of 16; a boy who was too young to fight but old enough to take everything the Marines could throw at him. He spent 10 years in the Marines during the years of 1979-1989.

Today, John lives in Nottingham, UK with his wife and one child. He spends a lot of time with his son, Charlie, playing ice hockey, speed skating, football and swimming.

As a commercial diver, he is now Diving Superintendent Offshore Manager working on Dive support vessels.

Lightning Source UK Ltd.
Milton Keynes UK
UKHW02f0309241217
314965UK00005B/292/P